روزه داری و قناعت هوسم بود ولی

چشمکی می زد آن مرغ و فنجان که مپرس

To fast and lead a frugal life
  Was all that I wished.
But the temptation of that Food of Life
  Is too much—do not ask!

Food of Life

*A Book of Ancient Persian and
Modern Iranian Cooking and Ceremonies*

NAJMIEH BATMANGLIJ

Mage Publishers, Inc.

Washington, D.C.

ACKNOWLEDGEMENTS

Calligraphy A.H. Tabnak
Cover photo Aldo Tutino
Sofreh-e Haft Sinn photo Jerome Adamstein
All other photos Serge
Bibliotheque Nationale, Paris
The American Schools of Oriental Research
Book design N. Batmanglij

SPECIAL THANKS TO

Gerry Cervenka
Darienne Moyer and Susan Derecskey
Joanne Nobile
Dana Pratt
Rosy and Florio
Neam's Market
Washington International School

خوشنویسی کتاب توسط امیر حسین تابناک

Published in French by Jacques Grancher as "Ma Cuisine d'Iran" in 1984.

Library of Congress Cataloging-in-Publication Data

Batmanglij, Najmieh.
    Food of life.

    Rev. translation of: Ma cuisine d'Iran.
    Includes index.
    1. Cookery, Iranian.   I. Title.
TX724.5.I7B3813   1986   641.5955   86-8333
ISBN 0-934211-00-0

This book may be purchased directly from the publisher.

Mage Publishers, Inc.
1032 29th St., N.W.
Washington, D.C. 20007
(202) 342-1642

Printed in the United States of America

I dedicate this book
to my sons Zal and Rostam.

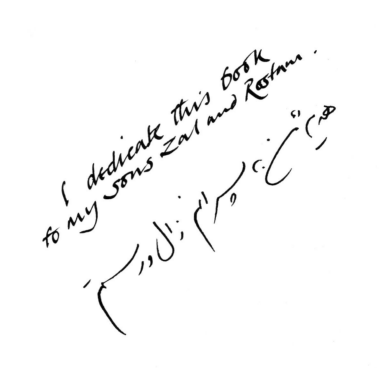

CONTENTS

ما لعبتکانیم و فلک لعبت باز   از روی حقیقت نه که از روی مجاز

بازیچه همی کنیم بر نطع وجود   افتیم بصندوق عدم یک یک باز

خیّام

We are playthings, and heaven is the player
In very truth, not metaphorically:
We play our little game on the board of existence, then we fall
Back one by one into the vault of non-existence.

Khayyam

PREFACE

When I am at home with the *samovar* steaming and the house fragrant with the smell of onions and garlic cooking, when the air is filled with the captivating aroma of mint and rare spices, what beautiful memories come back to me! I see the pantry behind the kitchen of my childhood home once again. The odors of savory, fenugreek, marjoram and angelica burst through the white cloth sacks that hang from the ceiling. Perhaps this book was inspired most by those perfumed memories.

Above all, though, the cuisine of my country brings back to me the image of my parents and friends sitting cross-legged on a Persian carpet around the *sofreh*, a cotton tablecloth embroidered with poems and prayers.

Iranians wake up early, before the sun rises. In our family, my father and grandmother engaged in an amusing little contest every morning. The first one up was the proud winner. As soon as he awoke, my father would usually go out into the garden and head straight for the jasmine we had growing in red clay pots. He would pick all the flowers that had bloomed overnight and lay them at my mother's place on the *sofreh*. But sometimes Grandmother would get to the garden first. I can still hear father speaking in that mock-angry tone of his as he discovered that the jasmine bushes had been stripped of their flowers. "That grandmother has been here already!" he would say out loud. When our grandmother nonchalantly joined the rest of the family at breakfast, she casually plucked the concealed flowers from their hiding place under her shawl and dropped the fragrant bouquet near my father. He would pretend to ignore her as he waited to take his sweet revenge the next morning.

I have fond memories of those breakfasts, or *sobhaneh*. The meal itself usually consists of sweet tea, feta cheese and *nan-e barbari*, a crusty, flat bread made fresh very early every morning. Breakfast sometimes includes other types of bread, jam and honey, fresh cream, butter and hot milk. Fried or soft-boiled eggs, saffron cake or pudding (*halva* or *sholeh zard*) might also be served or even, before a long mountain hike, a soup made of tripe (*sirab shirdoun*) and lamb head and feet (*kaleh patcheh*). *Sobhaneh* is a very important and pleasant moment in the life of an Iranian family, a time to be together before everyone leaves for work.

The cuisine of any country is a fundamental part of its heritage. The ingredients reflect its geography, while the savor and colors accent the aesthetic tastes of its inhabitants. And food is associated with so many major social events—births, weddings, funerals—that culinary traditions are intertwined with a country's history and religion. This is especially true of Iran (called "Persia" by westerners in ancient times).

Thousands of years ago, Zoroaster elaborated the ancient Indo-European myth of the Twins. One became good and the other evil, one the follower of truth and the other of falsehood. This concept of duality is typically Persian and it extends beyond moral issues. We often balance light and darkness, sweet and sour, hot and cold.

For us, food is also classified as "hot" (*garmi*), which thickens the blood and speeds the metabolism, and "cold" (*sardi*), which dilutes the blood and slows the metabolism. Dates, figs and grapes, for example, are hot fruits; plums, peaches and oranges are cold.

It takes a certain skill to correctly select food for the family, since people too can have hot and cold natures. An extremely out-of-balance diet can lead to illness. For example, those with "hot" natures must eat cold foods to achieve a balance. My son, like many other five-year-olds, sometimes eats too many dates or chocolates. Because he has a hot nature—something I learned very early in his life!—too much of this hot food does not agree with him at all. Drinking watermelon or grapefruit juice, or the nectar from other cold fruits, quickly helps restore his balance–and his smile.

Increasingly, science is discovering links between food and health. And while the ancient Persian system of balance does not eliminate the need for doctors, experience has proven that it is an excellent nutritional adjunct to good health.

My objective in writing this book was not just to compile a collection of recipes, however delicious they might be. Instead I have tucked in among them other pearls of wisdom from my country—verses from our poets and old legends. I have described an Iranian wedding and some of our joyful holiday traditions. I included photographs to show that our dishes are as colorful as our most beautiful carpets. For us, feasting our eyes is the first pleasure of a good meal.

I have always enjoyed cooking and have selected these recipes on the basis of my personal preferences and experience. I was aided in my research by my mother and other great cooks, who gave me valuable advice. As my knowledge grew, so did my curiosity and interest in my country's gastronomic heritage. This led me to research the origins of many of our ceremonies.

Among all the traditional recipes I have collected, only the simplest are included here. I have refined them over the years, first in France and then in the United States. In many instances, I have adapted old recipes to modern kitchen tools, like the food processor and the electric rice cooker. All the recipes were systematically tested using ingredients, which are now, because of the increasing Iranian expatriate community, available almost everywhere in America.

When I think of a meal, I think of the family all together. I hope that my sons will have similar memories of the simple pleasures of life when they are grown up. I dedicate this collection to them and to all Iranian children living far from the country of their heritage by the course of political events.

Najmieh Batmanglij
Georgetown, March 1986

دوش دیدم که ملائک در منحانه زدند   گل آدم بسرشتند و به پیمانه زدند

ساکنان حرم ستر و عفاف ملکوت   با من راه نشین باده مستانه زدند

حافظ

Last night I saw the angels knocking at the tavern door
Modeling the clay of man, becoming drunk with the original wine;
The inhabitants of the sacred enclosure and of the divine Malakut
Drank from one cup with me, the Pilgrim.

Hafiz

A P P E T I Z E R S

Eating-Matter and Reading-Matter

Mulla Nasrudin was carrying home some liver which he had just bought. In the other hand he had a recipe for liver pie which a friend had given him.

Suddenly a crow swooped down and carried off the liver. "You fool!" shouted Mulla, "the meat is all very well–but I still have the recipe."

مُخلّفات

Appetizers and Side Dishes

Traditionally, Iranian meals are served on the *sofreh*, a cotton cover embroidered with prayers and poems, which is spread over a Persian carpet or a table. The main dishes are surrounded with bread and a number of small bowls and relish dishes filled with appetizers and condiments. These are called *mokhalafatte*. Among them might be:

—a plate of raw vegetables and fresh herbs (radishes, scallions, mint, basil,
  parsley, tarragon, watercress) with feta cheese;
—peeled, sliced cucumbers;
—sweetened melon slices;
—peeled steamed beets;
—a basket of grapes;
—shelled nuts and raisins;
—butter with a bowl of powdered sugar and a bowl of honey;
—yogurt;
—*torshi* (Persian pickles, page 164);
—yogurt with spinach;
—cucumber salad with mint and vinegar;
—cucumber, tomato and onion salad;
—lemon juice, wine vinegar and olive oil.

All those sitting around the *sofreh* help themselves according to their fancy.

Bread and Cheese with Fresh Vegetables and Herbs

Nan-o Panir-o Sabzi-Khordan

No Persian table would be complete without *nan-o panir-o sabzi-khordan*, quite simply bread and fresh feta cheese with raw vegetables and herbs. The bread is spread with the feta cheese and garnished with raw vegetables and herbs.

Persian bread is called *nan* and there are several kinds. *Nan-e sangake* is a large, flat rectangular loaf arched on one end and about 3 feet long by 18 inches wide by 1 inch thick. It is baked in the oven on hot stones and served warm. *Nan-e lavash* is a very thin, crisp bread in a round or oval shape. It keeps well for several days. *Nan-e barbari* is a flat, oval loaf, about 2 inches thick. It should be eaten very fresh and warm; it is usually served for breakfast.

Panir is a cheese similar to feta cheese. It can be made from either cow's milk or goat's milk.

Sabzi-khordan is an assortment of raw vegetables and fresh herbs. It usually includes radishes, scallions and watercress with tarragon, mint, chives and basil. The vegetables and herbs are arranged on a platter with a piece of feta cheese.

Yogurt and Eggplant

Makes 4 servings
Preparation time: 15 min., plus
several hours refrigeration
Cooking time: 1 hr.

1 large or 2 small eggplants,
   about 1 pound
½ cup oil
1 onion, finely sliced
2 cloves garlic, crushed
1 cup plain yogurt
1 teaspoon salt

¼ teaspoon freshly ground
   pepper
1 tablespoon chopped fresh mint
   or 1 teaspoon dried mint

Borani-e Bademjan

1. Preheat oven to 350°F. Wash eggplant and prick with a fork to prevent bursting. Place whole eggplant on oven rack and bake for 1 hour.

2. Remove from oven, place on a cutting board and let stand until cool enough to handle. Peel and chop fine.

3. Heat the oil in a skillet and brown the onion and garlic. Add the eggplant and mix well. Season to taste with salt and pepper. Remove from heat and let cool.

4. Transfer to a serving dish, mix with yogurt and garnish with mint. Refrigerate for several hours before serving.

Yogurt and Spinach

Makes 4 servings
Preparation time: 10 min. plus
several hours refrigeration
Cooking time: 10 min.

1 cup fresh or frozen chopped spinach
2 onions, finely chopped
2 cloves garlic, crushed
4 tablespoons oil
1½ cups yogurt
½ teaspoon salt

¼ teaspoon freshly ground pepper
¼ teaspoon saffron dissolved in 1 tablespoon hot water

Borani-e Esfenaj

1. Place spinach in a pan, cover and steam until wilted, about 5 minutes. Drain.

2. In a skillet, brown onions and garlic in oil.

3. Stir in the spinach and cook for 2 minutes. Remove from heat and let cool.

4. In a serving bowl, mix yogurt and spinach and season to taste with salt and pepper. Garnish with dissolved saffron.

5. Refrigerate for several hours before serving.

Yogurt and Cooked Beets

2 large cooked beets, peeled, or 1 can (16 ounces) beets, drained
1 cup yogurt
1 tablespoon chopped fresh mint or ½ teaspoon dried mint

Makes 4 servings
Preparation time: 5 min.
Cooking time: 45 min. if fresh beets are used

Borani-e Labu

1. If using fresh beets, steam them with the skins for about 45 minutes.

2. Peel and cut cooked or canned beets into ¾-inch cubes.

3. Place yogurt in serving bowl and add the beets. Mix well. Garnish with mint and serve immediately.

Yogurt and Cucumber

Makes 6 servings
Preparation time: 15 min. plus 1 hr. chilling
Cooking time: none

1 long burpless cucumber
½ cup yellow raisins
3 cups yogurt
½ cup sour cream
¼ cup chopped scallions
1 tablespoon chopped mint
2 tablespoons chopped fresh dill weed
2 cloves garlic, crushed
3 tablespoons chopped walnuts
1 teaspoon salt
¼ teaspoon ground pepper
½ teaspoon chopped fresh or dried mint for garnish
1 dried rosebud and a few petals

Mast-o Khiar

1. Peel and grate cucumber.

2. Soak raisins in cold water for about 5 minutes. Drain.

3. In a serving bowl, combine yogurt, sour cream, cucumbers, scallions, mint, dill weed, garlic, chopped walnuts and raisins. Mix thoroughly and season to taste with salt and pepper.

4. Garnish with ½ teaspoon mint, the rosebud and petals.

5. Refrigerate for at least 1 hour before serving.

Variation: This may be transformed into a refreshing cold soup by adding 1 cup of cold water and 2 or 3 ice cubes to the mixture.

Yogurt and Shallots

4 shallots
2 cups yogurt
½ teaspoon salt
¼ teaspoon ground pepper

Makes 4 servings
Preparation time: 10 min. plus
overnight soaking and chilling
Cooking time: none

Mast-o Musir

1. Peel and chop shallots and soak in cold water overnight.

2. Drain the shallots and combine them with the yogurt, salt and pepper. Chill in refrigerator for several hours before serving.

Eggplant With Pomegranate

Makes 4 servings
Preparation time: 5 min.
Cooking time: 1 hr. 30 min.

2 medium eggplants
2 tomatoes, peeled and chopped
1 teaspoon lemon juice
2 tablespoons oil
1 onion, grated
2 cloves garlic, crushed
½ teaspoon salt
¼ teaspoon freshly ground
    pepper

1 teaspoon *gol-par* powder
    (angelica)
1 tablespoon chopped fresh mint
    or 1 teaspoon dried mint
1 tablespoon pomegranate paste

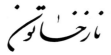

Nazkhatoune

1. To bake eggplants, prick them with a fork to prevent bursting and place on the rack of a preheated 350°F oven. Bake for 1 hour.

2. Place the eggplant on a cutting board and let stand until cool enough to handle. Peel and chop.

3. Put eggplant and tomatoes in a saucepan. Add lemon juice, oil, onion and garlic. Season with ½ teaspoon salt and ¼ teaspoon pepper. Sprinkle with *gol-par* powder and mint. Add pomegranate paste. Stir and simmer gently for 15 minutes. Taste for seasoning.

4. Pile in a serving dish and serve hot or cold.

Note: *Gol-par* powder is available at food specialty shops (page 240).

Tomato and Cucumber Salad

Makes 4 servings
Preparation time: 15 min.
Cooking time: none

2 firm ripe tomatoes
1 long burpless cucumber
3 tablespoons olive oil
  Juice of one lemon
1 clove garlic, crushed
½ teaspoon salt
¼ teaspoon freshly ground
  pepper
2 scallions, chopped

3 radishes, sliced
½ cup chopped parsley
¼ cup chopped fresh mint
¼ cup chopped fresh dill weed

سالاد گوجه خیار

Salad-e Gojeh Khiar

1. Drop tomatoes into scalding hot water. Remove immediately, peel and cut them in quarters. Peel and cut cucumber into 1-inch cubes.

2. Combine olive oil, lemon juice, garlic, salt and pepper to taste. Add tomatoes, cucumber and remaining ingredients and toss. Serve immediately.

Cucumber and Mint Salad

Makes 4 servings
Preparation time: 15 min.

1 cucumber
1 onion, chopped
1 tablespoon chopped fresh mint
   or 1 teaspoon dried mint
2 tablespoons vinegar
½ teaspoon salt
¼ teaspoon ground pepper

سالاد سرکه خیار

Serkeh-Khiar

1. Peel cucumber and chop into ¼-inch cubes.

2. Combine all ingredients in a bowl and mix thoroughly.

Dried Fruits and Nuts

Ajeel

Ajeel, the Persian mixture of dried fruits with roasted nuts and seeds, is a wonderful nibbling snack that appeals to children as well as adults and fits in at any time of day. Exactly what goes into it and in what proportions depends as much on what is at hand as on the taste of the person who is preparing it. Because it has an infinite number of forms, there can be no conventional recipe for *ajeel*; you have to invent your own. Among the dried fruits to choose from are figs, apricots, peaches, raisins and mulberries. Dried pears, prunes and currants can also be used. Nuts can include roasted hazelnuts, almonds, walnuts, pistachios, cashews, chick-peas, watermelon seeds and pumpkin seeds. Mix the fruits, nuts and seeds together and serve in a bowl. People help themselves to what they want, using their fingers. (*Ajeel* may also be called *shab-chareh*, which literally means "night grazing.")

Sweet Chick-pea Powder

2   **cups roasted chick-pea flour**
1   **cup confectioners sugar**

Makes 3 cups
Preparation time: 5 min.

Ghahoot

1. Mix together the chick-pea powder and sugar.

2. Pour in a bowl.

Note: Roasted chick-pea flour is available in Persian food specialty shops (page 240).

As children we loved ghahoot. *Today we make it for our children and help them eat it, sometimes with our hands and sometimes with spoons. The best way is to take a handful, tilt your head back and then let it pour into your mouth.*

Charcoal Roasted Corn on the Cob

3 tablespoons salt
2 quarts water
8 ears of corn, shucked

Makes 4 servings
Preparation time: 10 min.
Cooking time: 10 min.

Balal

1. Prepare charcoal fire and dissolve salt in warm water.

2. When the coals are ready, roast the corn on all sides, turning frequently.

3. Plunge roasted corn into salted water and serve immediately.

Balal *is a popular snack and* balal *vendors are a familiar sight on the streets of Persian towns and cities, like pretzel vendors in the United States or chestnut vendors in Paris.*

Peeled Walnuts

1 pound walnuts

Gerdoo

1. Shell the walnuts. If they are dried, wash them and soak in very hot water. Refrigerate overnight.

2. Remove the outer membrane from the walnuts and drop them in a large bowl of cold water.

3. Drain and sprinkle with salt to taste.

4. Serve *gerdoo* as a snack or as a side dish with feta cheese and pita bread.

Variation: You may also use fresh or dried almonds.

Peeled walnuts are usually prepared with fresh walnuts in season but it can be done with the dried walnuts that are available almost all year round. Like balal, gerdoo *is sold by street vendors in Iran.*

S O U P S   A N D   A S H E S

D u c k   S o u p

A relative came to see Mulla Nasrudin from the country, and brought a duck. Mulla was grateful and had the bird cooked and shared it with his guest.

Presently another visitor arrived. He was a friend, as he said, "of the man who gave you the duck." Mulla fed him as well.

This happened several times. Mulla's home had become like a restaurant for out-of-town visitors. Everyone was a friend removed of the original donor of the duck.

Finally Mulla was exasperated. One day there was a knock at the door and a stranger appeared. "I am the friend of the friend of the friend of the man who brought you the duck from the country," he said.

"Come in," said Nasrudin.

They seated themselves at the table, and Nasrudin asked his wife to bring the soup.

When the guest tasted it, it seemed to be nothing more than warm water. "What sort of soup is this?" he asked Mulla.

"That," said Mulla, "is the soup of the soup of the soup of the duck."

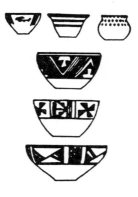

S o u p s   a n d   A s h e s

Soup plays a vital role in Iranian tradition. Many different kinds of soup are served to mark special occasions, and sharing a bowl of soup is believed to forge the bonds of friendship. Sometimes, in an act of great intimacy, close friends or lovers sip from the same spoon to seal their devotion. Some soups are thin, but many are thick and substantial enough to serve as a main course. "*Ashes*" (rhymes with squashes) are wonderfully flavorful thick soups. In Farsi, the cook is called *ashe-paz*, or the soup-preparer, and the kitchen is *ashe-paz khaneh*, the place where the soup is prepared. For best results, make the *ash* a day in advance to give the flavors a chance to meld and reheat it just before serving. Add the garnish at the last minute, after pouring the soup into the tureen. We Persians like to decorate our soups with various garnishes, creating patterns that are pleasing to the eye. Stir in the garnish just before serving, with warm crusty Persian or pita bread.

Lamb Shank Soup with Meat Paste

Makes 6 servings
Preparation time: 10 min.
Cooking time: 2 hrs.

2 pounds lamb shanks and 1 pound lamb breast
2 large onions, quartered
6 cups water
1 cup yellow split peas
1 teaspoon turmeric
2 teaspoons salt
½ teaspoon pepper
3 large potatoes, peeled and cut in halves
4 peeled tomatoes, garden-fresh, cut in halves

1 tablespoon tomato paste
2 teaspoons ground cinnamon
4 whole *limou-omani*, pierced, or ¼ cup lemon juice

GARNISH
1 large onion, thinly sliced
1 teaspoon ground cinnamon

Abgusht-e Lapeh-o-Gusht-e Kubideh

In this unique preparation, the cooked meat and vegetables are ground together to make a paste called gusht-e kubideh, *which is served with Persian pickles, raw vegetables and fresh herbs, and bread. The broth, embellished with marrow, is passed separately. Iranian cooks would use a mortar and pestle to pound the* gusht-e kubideh *to just the right consistency. A food processor may be used instead, but take care not to let the paste get too smooth and homogeneous.*

1. In a large pot, place the meat, onion and 6 cups of water. Bring to a boil, skimming the froth as it forms. Add split peas, turmeric, salt and pepper. Cover and let simmer 1½ hours over low heat.

2. Add the potatoes, tomatoes, tomato paste, cinnamon and *limou-omani* (pierce each lime first) or lemon juice. Simmer 30 minutes more over low heat.

3. Check to see if the meat and potatoes are done. Adjust seasoning.

4. Remove all of the stew ingredients, using a slotted spoon. Remove the meat from the bones. Mash the meat and vegetables together to make the paste called *gusht-e kubideh*. It should have the consistency of mashed potatoes. Season to taste with salt and pepper and arrange on a serving platter. Garnish with fresh slices of raw onion and sprinkle with cinnamon.

5. Reheat the broth and serve in a bowl as soup. Serve the *gusht-e kubideh* with *torshi* (Persian pickles, page 164), *sabzi-khordan* (a platter of scallions, radishes, fresh tarragon, basil and mint) and flat Iranian or pita bread.

Variations: 1. This soup may also be made with beef, cooking it for 1½ hours before adding the potatoes, or with veal (cooked 30 minutes before adding other ingredients). 2. One cup dried chick-peas or red kidney beans may be substituted for the split peas. 3. A peeled eggplant, sliced and sauteed in oil, may also be added with the potatoes and tomatoes.

Note: Limou-omani *(dried Persian limes) are available in food specialty shops (page 240).*

Lamb Shank Soup with Meat Paste
Abgusht-e Lapeh-o-Gusht-e Kubideh
page 24

Noodle Soup
Ash-e Reshteh
page 34

Lamb Shank Soup with Green Herbs

Makes 6 servings
Preparation time: 10 min.
Cooking time: 2 hrs.

2 pounds lamb shanks
2 onions, quartered
6 cups water
1 cup kidney beans
1 teaspoon turmeric
2 teaspoons salt
½ teaspoon freshly ground black pepper
1 cup chopped parsley
½ cup chopped scallions
1 tablespoon dried fenugreek leaves or 2 tablespoons fresh leaves, chopped

3 tablespoons oil
4 large potatoes, peeled and cut in chunks
3 whole *limou-omani*, pierced, or ¼ cup lemon juice
1 onion, finely sliced, for garnish

Abgusht-e Bozbash

1. In a large pot or large heavy Dutch oven, place meat, onions and 6 cups of water. Bring to a boil, skimming the froth as it forms. Add beans, turmeric, salt and pepper. Cover and simmer for 1 hour over low heat.

2. Saute parsley, scallions and fenugreek in 3 tablespoons oil and add to the soup. Cover and let simmer for ½ hour.

3. Add the potatoes and *limou-omani* (pierce each lime first) or lemon juice. Simmer 30 minutes longer.

4. Check to see if the meat and potatoes are done. Adjust seasoning.

5. Remove all of the stew ingredients, using a slotted spoon. Separate the meat from the bones and mash the meat and vegetables together to make the paste called *gusht-e kubideh*. Iranian cooks would use a mortar and pestle but a food processor may be used instead. Stop processing before the paste becomes fine and sticky. Season to taste with salt and pepper and pile it up on a platter. Garnish with onion slices.

6. Reheat the broth and serve separately as soup. Serve the *gusht-e kubideh* with *torshi* (Persian pickles, page 164) , *sabzi-khordan* (a platter of radishes, scallions, fresh tarragon, basil and mint) and pita bread.

This is another kind of Iranian soup, depending on parsley and scallions rather than tomatoes for its flavor. Here again the meat and vegetables are mashed together into a paste and served with fresh and pickled vegetables and flat bread.

Variations: This dish may also be made with veal or beef, either with the bone or with a piece of bone added to the pot for flavor.

Note: Limou-omani *(dried Persian limes) are available in food specialty shops (page 240).*

Pomegranate Soup

Makes 6 servings
Preparation time: 20 min.
Cooking time: 1 hr. 10 min.

4 onions
½ pound ground beef, veal or lamb
1 teaspoon salt
¼ teaspoon freshly ground black pepper
5 tablespoons oil
8 cups water
¼ cup yellow split peas
½ cup rice
1 cup chopped parsley
1 cup chopped coriander leaves

½ cup chopped scallions
½ cup fresh or frozen chopped spinach
¼ cup pomegranate paste or 1 cup pomegranate juice or 2 cups pomegranate seeds
⅓ cup sugar
2 teaspoons *gol-par* powder (angelica powder)
3 cloves garlic, crushed
1 teaspoon dried mint flakes

Ash-e Anar

1. Grate 1 of the onions and add to the meat in a bowl. Season to taste with salt and pepper. Mix ingredients thoroughly and shape into chestnut-size meatballs.

2. Finely slice the remaining 3 onions. Heat 3 tablespoons of the oil in a large heavy pot and brown the onions. Add 8 cups water and split peas. Bring to a boil, reduce heat and simmer over medium heat for 20 minutes.

3. Add the rice and 1 teaspoon salt and cook 15 minutes longer, stirring from time to time.

4. Add the chopped parsley, coriander, scallions and spinach and continue cooking for 20 minutes longer, stirring occasionally to prevent sticking.

5. Stir in pomegranate paste, sugar and *gol-par* powder. Add the meatballs and simmer over low heat for 35 minutes.

6. Check a meatball to see if it is done and taste soup for seasoning. Add water if the soup is too thick.

7. Just before serving, reheat the soup. Heat the remaining two tablespoons of oil in a skillet and brown the garlic. Remove from heat. Crumble the dried mint flakes in the palm of your hand and add to the garlic.

8. Pour soup into a tureen and garnish with the mint and garlic mixture.

Note: Pomegranate paste and *gol-par* powder are available in food specialty stores (page 240).

Beggar's Soup

Makes 8 servings
Preparation time: 20 min.
Cooking time: 2 hrs.

3 onions
4 tablespoons oil
1 pound beef, lamb or veal for stew, cut in ½-inch cubes
1 teaspoon turmeric
2 teaspoons salt
¼ teaspoon freshly ground pepper
12 cups water
⅓ cup dried red kidney beans
½ cup lentils

¼ cup dried chick-peas
¼ cup mung beans
¼ cup rice
½ cup chopped parsley
¼ cup chopped fresh dill
½ cup fresh or frozen chopped spinach
¼ cup chopped chives or scallions
3 cloves garlic, crushed

Ash-e Sholeh Ghalamkar

1. Chop 2 of the onions and brown them in 3 tablespoons oil in a large heavy pot. Push to one side and brown meat. Add turmeric, salt, ¼ teaspoon pepper and 12 cups water.

2. Add kidney beans, lentils, chickpeas and mung beans. Cover and simmer for 1 hour over low heat.

3. Add rice. Cook 20 minutes longer.

4. Add parsley, dill, spinach and chives. Cook 40 minutes longer, stirring occasionally to avoid sticking.

5. Check to be sure meat and beans are done and adjust seasoning. Add water if needed.

6. Just before serving, slice remaining onion and fry it in 1 tablespoon oil until golden brown; add crushed garlic. This takes about 20 minutes. Reheat the soup and pour into a tureen. Garnish with fried onion and garlic and serve.

Long ago, people used to leave a soup kettle by the side of the road to make a wish come true. Passers-by would throw in a few coins to be used to buy the ingredients for a soup. The more people pitched in, the better the chances of the wish coming true. Thus was born beggar's soup. Today, although kettles are no longer left at the roadside (perhaps for fear they would disappear!), the custom lives on in a new form. Friends are told in advance on what day a wish is going to be made. That morning, each one arrives bringing a few ingredients that can go into the soup. They prepare it together and sit down to share it at the midday meal. This way everyone can join in making a dear friend's wish come true.

Barley Soup

Makes 6 servings
Preparation time: 20 min.
Cooking time: 2 hrs. 30 min.

3 onions, finely chopped
½ pound boneless leg of lamb or beef, cut in ½-inch cubes
½ cup oil
2 teaspoons salt
½ teaspoon pepper
1 teaspoon turmeric
10 cups water
¼ cup dried red kidney beans (optional)
¼ cup dried chick-peas (optional)
¼ cup lentils
1 cup barley

¼ cup rice
½ cup chopped parsley
½ cup fresh coriander, chopped
½ cup fresh dill, chopped
1 cup fresh or frozen chopped spinach
1 cup liquid *kashke* or sour cream or yogurt

Garnish
3 cloves garlic, crushed
1 teaspoon dried mint leaves

Ash-e Jow

1. Brown 2 onions and meat in ⅓ cup oil in a large pot. Sprinkle with 2 teaspoons salt, ¼ teaspoon pepper and the turmeric. Pour in 10 cups of water and add kidney beans, chick-peas and lentils. Bring to a boil, reduce heat and cover. Simmer for 50 minutes over medium heat, stirring occasionally.

2. Add barley and rice. Cook 50 minutes longer, stirring occasionally.

3. Add parsley, coriander, dill and spinach and cook 50 minutes more.

4. Check to see that meat and beans are done. Adjust seasoning and add more water if needed.

5. Stir in the liquid *kashke*, stirring constantly for 5 minutes with a wooden spoon to prevent curdling. If you are using sour cream, let the soup cool first. Then blend 2 or 3 tablespoons of soup into the sour cream; slowly pour the mixture back into the soup.

6. Just before serving, reheat the soup to a simmer and prepare the garnish. Pour the rest of the oil into a small frying pan and brown the remaining onion and the garlic. Remove from heat. Crush dried mint in the palm of your hand and add to the oil and garlic.

7. Pour soup into tureen. Garnish with mint and garlic mixture.

Note: *Kashke* is whey. Liquid whey is sometimes available in specialty food shops (page 240), but the quality is often poor. I recommend using sour cream instead.

Cream of Barley Soup

Makes 6 servings
Preparation time: 20 min.
Cooking time: 1 hr. 25 min.

2 chopped onions
2 cloves of garlic, crushed
2 tablespoons oil
4 cups water
½ cup barley
2 cups homemade beef broth
1 carrot, grated
2 leeks, chopped fine
1 teaspoon salt
¼ teaspoon freshly ground black pepper
½ cup sour cream

Zest of ½ lemon
Juice of one lemon
2 tablespoons chopped parsley for garnishing

BEEF BROTH
1 pound beef shank
1 onion, chopped
4 cups water

Soup-e Jow

1. In a pot, brown onions and garlic in oil, then add 4 cups water, barley, 1 teaspoon salt and ¼ teaspoon pepper. Bring to a boil, reduce heat and simmer, covered, for 1 hour or until barley is done, stirring occasionally.

2. Remove some of the ingredients with a slotted spoon, reserving the broth in a pot, and puree the solids, using a food mill, blender or food processor. Return the puree to the soup.

3. To make the beef broth, combine the beef shank, 1 chopped onion and 4 cups water in a pot. Cover and let simmer over low heat for about 1 hour. Use the broth for the soup.

4. Add the beef broth, carrot and leek to the soup. Cook for 20 minutes.

5. Add the sour cream, lemon juice, and correct seasoning to your taste, adding more salt, pepper or lemon juice.

6. Just before serving, add chopped parsley and zest of lemon to the soup.

Mung Bean Soup

Makes 6 servings
Preparation time: 20 min.
Cooking time: 1 hr. 50 min.

3 onions, thinly sliced
½ cup oil
2 teaspoons salt
¼ teaspoon freshly ground black pepper
½ teaspoon turmeric
10 cups water
1 cup mung beans
½ cup rice
1 cup diced turnip
1 cup diced pumpkin meat
½ cup fresh coriander, chopped
1 cup chopped parsley
½ cup fresh dill, chopped

½ cup chopped scallions
1 cup pearl onions

GHEIMEH GARNISH
¼ pound stew lamb or beef, in ½-inch dice
1 small onion, chopped
3 cloves garlic, crushed
2 tablespoons yellow split peas
1 teaspoon tomato paste
¼ teaspoon saffron, dissolved in 1 tablespoon hot water
¼ teaspoon salt

Ash-e Mash

This hearty winter soup, in which turnips, winter squash and pearl onions are added to a mung-bean base, is subtly perfumed with saffron from the garnish we call gheimeh.

1. In a large Dutch oven, brown onions in ⅓ cup oil. Add salt, pepper and turmeric. Pour in 10 cups water. Add the mung beans. Bring to a boil, reduce heat and simmer 50 minutes, stirring from time to time and skimming off the skins if necessary.

2. Add rice, turnip, pumpkin meat, coriander, parsley, dill, scallions and pearl onions. Simmer gently for 1 hour, stirring occasionally.

3. Check to see if beans and vegetables are done, adjust seasoning and add more water if needed. Continue cooking if necessary until done.

4. About ½ hour before serving, prepare the *gheimeh* mixture as follows. Brown the meat with the chopped onion and garlic in the rest of the oil. Add split peas and ½ cup hot water. Simmer for 20 minutes. Add tomato paste, saffron and salt and simmer covered for 10 minutes more.

5. Pour soup into tureen. Decorate the surface of the soup with *gheimeh*. Stir it in just before ladling soup into individual bowls.

Note: Mung beans are tiny gray-green beans that are usually forced to germinate for bean sprouts. They are available in specialty food stores (page 240).

Yogurt Soup

Makes 6 servings
Preparation time: 40 min.
Cooking time: 1 hr. 45 min.

2 large onions
½ pound lean ground beef or chicken giblets, chopped
2 teaspoons salt
½ teaspoon freshly ground black pepper
½ cup oil
¼ teaspoon turmeric
10 cups water
¼ cup chick-peas or yellow split peas
½ cup lentils
½ cup rice
½ cup chopped parsley

½ cup chopped coriander
½ cup chopped scallions
3 sprigs fresh tarragon
1 cup chopped dill
5 sprigs spinach, washed, trimmed and chopped
3 chopped turnips
2 cups yogurt

GARNISH
3 cloves of garlic, minced
1 teaspoon dried mint flakes

Ash-e Mast

1. Grate 1 of the onions and combine with meat in a bowl. Season with ½ teaspoon salt and ¼ teaspoon pepper. Mix and shape into chestnut-size meatballs.

2. Chop remaining onion and brown it in ⅓ cup oil in a large pot. Add 1½ teaspoons salt, ¼ teaspoon pepper and turmeric. Pour in 10 cups water and add the chick-peas or yellow split peas and lentils. Cover and simmer for 35 minutes over medium heat.

3. Add rice and meatballs or chicken giblets and simmer 25 minutes more.

4. Add chopped herbs, spinach and turnips and cook another 50 minutes, stirring occasionally.

5. Check to see if peas and meatballs or chicken giblets are done and adjust seasoning. Cook a bit longer if necessary.

6. Add yogurt, stirring constantly for 5 minutes to prevent curdling.

7. Just before serving, reheat soup and prepare garnish by browning garlic in remaining oil in a small fry pan. Remove from heat. Crush mint flakes in the palm of your hand and add to the pan.

8. Pour soup into tureen. Pour mint and garlic mixture on top.

Note: This soup is an excellent remedy for a cold.

Sweet And Sour Soup

Makes 6 servings
Preparation time: 40 min.
Cooking time: 2 hrs. 5 min.

3 onions
½ pound ground beef or lamb
2½ teaspoons salt
½ teaspoon freshly ground black pepper
½ teaspoon cinnamon
½ cup oil
½ teaspoon turmeric
10 cups water
½ cup yellow split peas
½ cup rice
1 cup dried pitted prunes
1 cup dried apricots

¼ cup chopped walnuts
1 cup chopped parsley
¼ cup chopped chives or scallions
3 sprigs fresh mint, chopped
¼ cup sugar
¼ cup red wine vinegar

GARNISH
3 cloves garlic, crushed
1 teaspoon dried mint flakes

Ash-e Miveh

1. Grate 1 onion and combine with ground meat in a bowl. Add ½ teaspoon salt, ¼ teaspoon pepper and cinnamon. Mix well and shape into meatballs the size of a walnut.

2. Thinly slice the remaining onions and brown them in ⅓ cup oil in a large pot. Sprinkle with 2 teaspoons salt, ¼ teaspoon pepper and turmeric. Pour in 10 cups water and add the split peas. Cover and simmer for 25 minutes over medium heat, stirring occasionally.

3. Add rice and simmer 25 minutes longer.

4. Add prunes and cook 15 minutes more.

5. Add meatballs, apricots, walnuts, parsley, chives or scallions and fresh mint. Simmer 45 minutes over low heat.

6. Mix the sugar and vinegar together and stir into the soup. Cook 15 minutes or until done.

7. Adjust seasoning and add more sugar or vinegar to taste. Add more water if necessary.

8. Shortly before serving, brown garlic in remaining oil in a small frying pan. Remove from heat. Crush the mint flakes in the palm of your hand and add.

9. Pour soup into tureen. Pour garlic and mint garnish on top.

Onion Soup

Makes 6 servings
Preparation time: 20 min.
Cooking time: 40 min.

4 onions, finely sliced
½ cup oil
2 tablespoons flour
2 tablespoons dried fenugreek
1 teaspoon turmeric
6 cups water
3 potatoes, peeled and cut in halves

1 teaspoon salt
¼ teaspoon freshly ground black pepper
3 eggs

Eshkeneh

1. In a large pot, brown onions in ½ cup oil. This will take about 15 minutes. Add flour, fenugreek and turmeric. Stir constantly for 1 minute with a wooden spoon. Add 6 cups water, potatoes, 1 teaspoon salt and ¼ teaspoon pepper. Cook for 35 minutes over medium heat. Taste and correct seasoning. Check to see if the potatoes are done.

2. Add eggs. Stir for 5 minutes with wooden spoon.

3. Pour soup into tureen and eat with yogurt and bread.

Noodle Soup

Makes 6 servings
Preparation time: 20 min., plus
soaking the dried vegetables
Cooking time: 1 hr. 50 min.

¼ cup dried red kidney beans
¼ cup navy beans
¼ cup chick-peas
3 onions, finely sliced
½ cup oil
2 teaspoons salt
½ teaspoon freshly ground black pepper
1 teaspoon turmeric
10 cups water
½ cup lentils
1 cup home made beef broth
½ cup coarsely chopped chives or scallions
½ cup coarsely chopped parsley
2 cups fresh or frozen chopped spinach
1 beet, peeled and diced in ½-inch pieces
½ pound flat egg noodles (Reshteh)
1 cup liquid *kashke* or sour cream or ¼ cup wine vinegar

GHEIMEH GARNISH
¼ pound beef, in ½-inch cubes
1 small onion, chopped
3 cloves garlic, crushed
2 tablespoons oil
½ cup water
2 tablespoons yellow split peas
1 teaspoon tomato paste
¼ teaspoon saffron, dissolved in 1 tablespoon hot water
½ teaspoon salt

MINT GARNISH
1 onion, finely sliced
3 cloves of garlic, crushed
1 tablespoon oil
1 teaspoon dried mint flakes

Ash-e Reshteh

We Iranians always eat noodles before embarking on something new. For us they symbolize the choice of paths among the many that life spreads out before us. Eating those tangled strands is like unraveling the Gordian knot of life's infinite possibilities in order to pick out the best. Noodles, we believe, can bring good fortune and make new endeavors fruitful. That is why noodles are always served on *Norouz*, the Iranian New Year's Day. Another traditional occasion is on the third day after friends or relatives have gone away on a trip. It is believed that by eating noodles we can send them luck as they follow the path of their journey.

1. Soak the beans and chick-peas for 2 hours if desired. Lentils do not need to be soaked.

2. Brown the onions in 3 tablespoons oil in a large pot. Add 2 teaspoons salt, ¼ teaspoon pepper and turmeric. Pour in 10 cups water and add drained kidney beans, navy beans and chick-peas. Cover and simmer for 45 minutes.

3. Add lentils and beef broth. Cook 35 minutes longer.

4. Add chopped scallions, parsley, spinach and the beet. Continue cooking, stirring from time to time, for 20 minutes or until done. Correct seasoning and add more water if the soup is too thick.

5. Add noodles and cook until done, about 10 minutes, stirring occasionally.

6. Stir in the *kashke* or sour cream or vinegar. If sour cream or *kashke* is used, first set aside a heaping tablespoonful for garnish. Stir 2 tablespoons of soup into the sour cream. Pour this mixture slowly back into the soup. Reheat just before serving.

7. About ½ hour before serving, prepare the *gheimeh* garnish. Brown the meat, onion and garlic in 2 tablespoons of oil. Stir in ½ cup of water and the split peas; cover and cook for 20 minutes over low heat. Add the tomato paste, saffron and ½ teaspoon salt and simmer, covered, for 10 minutes.

8. While the *gheimeh* garnish is simmering, prepare the mint garnish. Brown the onion and garlic in 3 tablespoons oil in a frying pan. Remove from heat. Crush mint flakes in palm of your hand and mix them in.

9. Pour soup into tureen. Garnish with *gheimeh* and mint garnish and the reserved dollop of sour cream.

Note: *Kashke* is whey. Liquid whey is available in food specialty stores but since the quality is not always good, I use sour cream instead. *Reshteh* (Persian noodles) are also available at Middle Eastern food shops (page 240).

Mint Soup

Makes 6 servings
Preparation time: 20 min.
Cooking time: 25 min.

3 onions, 1 grated and 2 thinly
  chopped
⅓ cup oil
1 tablespoon mint flakes
¼ cup chopped walnuts
1 teaspoon turmeric
1 teaspoon salt

½ teaspoon freshly ground black
  pepper
4 cups water
2 cups liquid *kashke* (whey) or
  sour cream

Kalleh Joosh

1. In a Dutch oven, brown chopped onions in ⅓ cup oil. Sprinkle with half the mint flakes and all but 2 tablespoons of the nuts. Stir and cook 2 minutes.

2. Add turmeric, 1 teaspoon salt, ½ teaspoon pepper and 4 cups water. Bring to a boil, reduce heat and simmer over medium heat for 20 minutes.

3. Slowly stir in *kashke*. If you are using sour cream, pour some soup in the sour cream, blend thoroughly and then pour the mixture back in the soup. Taste and adjust seasoning. If using *kashke*, reduce the salt. Reheat to a simmer before serving.

4. Garnish soup with remaining mint flakes and walnuts.

Note: *Kashke* is whey. It is available in both dried and liquid form in food specialty shops (page 240). Since the quality of liquid whey is not always good, I use sour cream instead.

Lamb's Head and Feet Soup

Makes 4 servings
Preparation time: 30 min.
Cooking time: 4 hrs.

1 mutton or lamb's head with the tongue
6 cups water
4 mutton or lambs feet or 2 shanks
2 large onions, quartered
4 cloves garlic
2 bay leaves

½ teaspoon freshly ground black pepper
2 teaspoons salt
1 teaspoon cinnamon
1 teaspoon turmeric
Croutons

Kalleh Pacheh

Traditionally, kalleh pacheh *is made with the head (including the tongue) and the feet of a mutton or lamb. Shanks may be substituted for the feet, which are not available everywhere. The head can be ordered from butcher shops with a Greek or Middle Eastern clientele. Lamb's head and feet soup has a surprisingly delicate flavor that is best set off with* torshi *(Persian pickles, page 164).*

1. Sear mutton head and feet over open flame to burn off hairs. Scrape and wash thoroughly. Remove the nose completely. Split the head in half vertically, with the tongue in one half, unless the butcher has already done so. Rinse with cold water.

2. Bring 6 cups water to a boil and add the head, tongue and the feet or shanks as well as the onions, garlic and bay leaves. Slowly bring to a simmer, skimming froth as it forms. When it stops forming, cover and simmer over low heat for 4 hours or until meat separates easily from bones. Skim broth occasionally while cooking. Add water if necessary to keep level at a minimum of 3 cups.

3. Remove the head from the soup and separate the meat and brains from the bones of the skull. Peel the tongue and cut it into bite-size pieces. Return meat to broth.

4. Season to taste with pepper and salt, cinnamon and turmeric. Do not add salt until soup is cooked to prevent ingredients from discoloring.

5. Pour soup into a tureen. Place croutons in each soup bowl before ladling out the soup. Serve with lots of *torshi* (Persian pickles, page 164) and *sabzi-khordan* (fresh vegetables and herbs).

Tripe Soup

Makes 4 servings
Preparation time: 20 min.
Cooking time: 4 hrs.

1   **pound calf or lamb tripe (see note below)**
2   **large onions, quartered**
2   **cloves garlic**
2   **whole bay leaves**
6   **cups water**
¼   **teaspoon freshly ground black pepper**
1   **teaspoon salt**

Sirab Shir-Doun

1. Clean and wash tripe. Cut into small pieces.

2. Place tripe, onions, garlic and bay leaves in a large pot. Add 6 cups water.

3. Cover and simmer over low heat for 3–4 hours or until meat separates easily. Skim broth occasionally while cooking. Add water if necessary to keep level at a minimum of 3 cups.

4. Season to taste with ¼ teaspoon pepper and 1 teaspoon salt. Do not add salt until cooking is finished as it might discolor the tripe.

5. Pour into a tureen and serve with *torshi* (Persian pickles, page 164), a platter of raw vegetables and fresh herbs, and bread.

Note: Cleaned tripe is available at various ethnic butchers and some supermarkets (see page 240). It may be necessary to order it in advance.

VEGETABLES

Unless we clap hands together in unison, we shall
  Not stamp feet in joy upon the head of sorrow:
Let us drink a morning cup before the hour of dawn,
  For this dawn will often break when we no longer
Breathe.

Omar Khayyam

تا دست با اتّفاق درهم نزنیم

پائ نشاط بر سر غم نزنیم

پیش از که صبحدم صبوحی نزنیم

کین صبح بسی دمد که ما دم نزنیم

خیّام

V e g e t a b l e s

Persians rarely eat plain vegetables as side dishes. Instead, vegetables are often combined with beans, grains and fruit or stuffed with fruits, rice and meats.

We are very partial to these stuffed vegetables, called *dolmeh*. Some favorite vegetables for *dolmeh* are grape and cabbage leaves, eggplant, zucchini and tomatoes. Fruits like quinces and apples are also used. Generally speaking, *dolmeh* may be served cold as an appetizer or hot as a main dish accompanied with bread and yogurt.

The good cook always chooses vegetables in season, when they are at their height in flavor and nutritional value. Herbs vary in intensity even from season to season. For example, the perfume of dill in spring is strongest and most desirable for cooking. Garden-fresh fruits, vegetables and herbs should be used whenever possible. They give superior results in every way.

Stuffed Grape Leaves

Makes 6 servings
Preparation time: 55 min.
Cooking time: 1 hr. 30 min.

50 fresh grape leaves, in season, or 51 canned leaves
⅔ cup rice
¼ cup yellow split peas
1 teaspoon salt
1 cup chopped scallions
½ cup fresh chopped dill
3 sprigs fresh tarragon, chopped
3 sprigs fresh mint, chopped
½ cup chopped parsley

½ pound ground meat (lamb, veal or beef)
   Juice of 3 lemons
¼ teaspoon freshly ground black pepper
1 teaspoon ground cinnamon
¼ cup oil or butter
2 tablespoons sugar

Dolmeh-e Barg-e Mo

Note: *Canned grape leaves are available in specialty food shops (page 240) and sometimes on the gourmet shelf of the supermarket.*

1. If fresh grape leaves are used, pick small and tender ones, blanch them in boiling water for 2 minutes, then drain in a colander and rinse with cold water. For canned grape leaves, drain in a colander and rinse under running water.

2. In a saucepan, cook rice and split peas for 20 minutes over medium heat in 3 cups of water. Add ½ teaspoon salt and drain in a colander.

3. In a bowl, combine chopped scallions, dill, tarragon, mint, parsley, rice and split peas, meat, and the juice of 1 lemon. Season with ½ teaspoon salt, pepper and cinnamon. Mix thoroughly, using hands or a wooden spoon.

4. Place three layers of grape leaves at the bottom of a well-oiled shallow ovenproof dish.

5. Place two grape leaves one on top of the other in the palm of one hand. Top with 1 tablespoon stuffing. Roll up the leaves, folding in the ends to prevent stuffing from leaking out while cooking. Place in dish.

6. Pour in 2 cups water and ¼ cup oil. Set an ovenproof plate on top of the stuffed grape leaves. Cover it and bake in preheated 350°F oven for 1 hour.

7. Mix 2 tablespoons sugar with the juice of 2 lemons. Remove dish from oven and sprinkle with this sauce. Cover and return to oven. Bake an additional 30 minutes.

8. When the grape leaves are tender, taste sauce and adjust seasoning. The sauce should be quite thick. Serve in the same baking dish or on a platter, while hot or warm, with bread and yogurt.

Stuffed Cabbage Leaves

Makes 4 servings
Preparation time: 1 hr.
Cooking time: 1 hr. 15 min.

1 large head of green cabbage
¼ cup rice
¼ cup yellow split peas
1 onion, finely chopped
1 pound ground meat (lamb, veal or beef)
¼ cup oil or butter
2 tablespoons tomato paste
¼ cup chopped parsley
2 tablespoons chopped mint

2 tablespoons chopped dill
1 tablespoon chopped tarragon
1 teaspoon salt
¼ teaspoon freshly ground black pepper
½ teaspoon cinnamon
⅓ cup sugar
⅓ cup vinegar or lemon juice

Dolmeh-e Kalam

1. Core cabbage and remove individual leaves. Wash and plunge into boiling salted water. Cover and boil for 5 minutes, drain in colander and rinse under cold water.

2. Cook rice and split peas in 2 cups water for 30 minutes. Drain.

3. Brown onion and meat in ¼ cup oil. Add tomato paste and mix thoroughly.

4. Combine meat, rice and split peas and chopped herbs in a large bowl. Season with salt, pepper and cinnamon. Mix well.

5. Place a cabbage leaf in the palm of one hand. Top with 1 tablespoon stuffing. Roll tightly, folding in the sides of the leaves to prevent stuffing from leaking out while cooking.

6. Place 2 layers of the remaining cabbage leaves in a well greased ovenproof dish. Arrange stuffed cabbage leaves side by side on top. Pour in 1½ cups water. Cover and bake in a preheated 350°F oven for 45 minutes.

7. Combine sugar and vinegar or lemon juice. Pour mixture into baking dish. Return to oven, cover and bake 30 minutes more. Baste stuffed cabbage leaves occasionally with pan juices.

8. When the stuffed cabbage is done, taste sauce and adjust seasoning by adding more vinegar or sugar. Serve in same baking dish with bread and yogurt on the side.

Stuffed Green Peppers, Eggplants and Tomatoes

Makes 4 servings
Preparation time: 45 min.
Cooking time: 1 hr. 20 min.

*Dolmeh-e Felfel
Sabz-o Bademjan-o
Gojeh Farangi*

4 large tomatoes
2 green bell peppers
2 eggplants or pattypan squash
¼ cup rice
¼ cup yellow split peas
½ cup oil
1 onion, finely chopped
1 pound ground beef, lamb or veal
2 tablespoons tomato paste
¼ cup chopped parsley

1 tablespoon chopped mint
1 tablespoon chopped tarragon
1 tablespoon chopped scallions
1 teaspoon salt
¼ teaspoon freshly ground black pepper
1 teaspoon cinnamon
⅓ cup vinegar or lemon juice
⅓ cup sugar

1. Wash tomatoes, green peppers and eggplants.

2. Remove stems from eggplants. Slice off the tops, remove caps and set aside. Slice off the bottoms so the eggplants can stand on their own. Hollow out using the point of a knife and a teaspoon and discard the eggplant flesh. Sprinkle the shells with 1 tablespoon salt and place in a colander to drain for 20 minutes.

3. Cut off the tops of the green peppers ½ inch from the stem and set caps aside. Blanch peppers for 5 minutes in boiling water. Rinse in cold water and drain.

4. Remove stems from tomatoes. Cut a slice off the tops, remove caps and set aside. Remove tomato flesh using a teaspoon and set aside.

5. Cook rice and split peas together for 20 minutes in 2 cups water and ¼ teaspoon salt. Drain.

6. Rinse eggplants and pat dry. Brown on all sides in 3 tablespoons hot oil, adding more if necessary. Set aside.

7. Brown onion and meat in 2 tablespoons oil. Stir in 1 tablespoon tomato paste.

8. In a large bowl, combine meat, rice and split peas and the chopped herbs. Season with 1 teaspoon salt and ¼ teaspoon pepper. Mix thoroughly.

9. Fill tomatoes, green peppers and eggplants with stuffing. Replace caps.

10. Place the stuffed peppers and eggplants side by side in an ovenproof dish, leaving room for the tomatoes, which do not need to cook as long. Mix 1 tablespoon tomato paste in 2 cups water or broth and pour around the stuffing. Cover and bake in a preheated 350°F oven for 45 minutes.

11. Combine the tomato pulp, cinnamon, 2 tablespoons oil, lemon juice and sugar. Mix well.

12. Remove the dish from the oven and add the stuffed tomatoes. Pour the tomato-pulp mixture around the stuffed vegetables, cover and return to oven. Bake for 35 minutes longer or more.

13. When the vegetables are done, taste the sauce and correct seasoning. Serve in baking dish or arrange on a platter. Serve with bread and yogurt.

Stuffed Potatoes

Makes 3 servings
Preparation time: 45 min.
Cooking time: 1 hr.

5 large potatoes, about 1 pound
½ cup oil
1 onion, finely chopped
½ pound ground meat (lamb, veal or beef)
3 tablespoons tomato paste
½ cup chopped parsley
2 eggs
1 teaspoon salt
¼ teaspoon of freshly ground black pepper

Dolmeh-e Sibzamini

1. Wash and peel potatoes. Cut off tops and set aside. Slice off the bottoms so the potatoes can stand up straight. Hollow out potatoes with a potato peeler or a teaspoon, leaving a shell ½ inch thick.

2. Brown potatoes in a skillet in ¼ cup oil.

3. Brown onion and meat in remaining oil. Add 1 tablespoon tomato paste, parsley, beaten eggs, salt and pepper. Mix thoroughly for 3 minutes and remove from heat.

4. Fill potatoes with stuffing, replace tops and arrange in an ovenproof dish.

5. Dilute remaining tomato paste in 1 cup water. Pour mixture over and around potatoes in baking dish. Cover and bake in a preheated 350°F oven for 1 hour. Baste occasionally with pan juices.

6. Check to see if potatoes are done and adjust seasoning. Serve in same baking dish or arrange on a platter. Serve with bread, fresh herbs and *torshi* (Persian pickles, page 164).

Stuffed Quince or Apple

Makes 6 servings
Preparation time: 45 min.
Cooking time: 1 hr. 30 min.

4 large quinces similar in size or
  8 baking apples
¼ cup yellow split peas or ¼ cup
  green peas
1 onion, finely chopped
½ pound ground meat (lamb, veal
  or beef)
¼ cup oil
1 teaspoon tomato paste
⅓ cup vinegar or lemon juice

2 teaspoons salt
¼ teaspoon pepper
1 teaspoon cinnamon
¼ cup sugar
1 tablespoon butter
¼ teaspoon saffron, dissolved in
  1 tablespoon hot water

دلمه به یا سیب

*Dolmeh-e Beh ya
Sib*

1. Wash quinces or apples. Cut off tops of fruit and hollow out, using the tip of a knife to scoop out the seeds and some of the pulp, leaving ½ inch of pulp on all sides. Set tops aside.

2. Cook split peas in 2 cups water for 30 minutes over medium heat. Drain. Or cook green peas in ¼ cup water for 10 minutes and drain.

3. Brown onion and meat in 2 tablespoons oil. Add tomato paste, 2 tablespoons vinegar or lemon juice, split peas or green peas, 1½ teaspoons salt, pepper and cinnamon. Mix thoroughly.

4. Fill quinces with stuffing, replace tops and place in a well-greased ovenproof dish.

5. Combine 1 cup water with the remaining vinegar or lemon juice, sugar, ½ teaspoon salt, 1 tablespoon butter and saffron. Pour over the fruit into baking dish. Cover and place in a preheated 350°F oven. Bake 1½ hours for quince, about 1 hour for apples, basting occasionally with pan juices.

6. Check to see if fruit is done and adjust seasonings. Serve in same baking dish or arrange on a platter. Serve with bread, yogurt and fresh herbs.

Eggplant Puree

Makes 6 servings
Preparation time: 20 min.
Cooking time: 2 hrs.

1 pound boned lamb shank, veal or beef
2 onions, finely chopped
½ cup oil or butter
2 cups lentils
2 teaspoons salt
½ teaspoon freshly ground black pepper
2 medium eggplants
2 cups sour cream or 1 cup liquid whey (*kashke*)

GARNISH
2 tablespoons oil or butter
1 onion, finely chopped
2 cloves garlic, crushed
2 tablespoons dried mint
3–4 walnut halves
1 tablespoon sour cream or liquid whey (*kashke*)
¼ teaspoon saffron dissolved in 1 tablespoon hot water

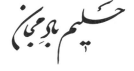

Halime Bademjan

1. Cut meat into small pieces and brown with onions in 3 tablespoons oil. Add 4 cups water, the lentils, 2 teaspoons salt and the pepper. Bring to a boil, skimming froth as it forms. Cover and simmer over low heat for 1 hour or until very tender.

2. Peel eggplants. Slice lengthwise. Sprinkle with 1 teaspoon salt and let stand for 20 minutes. Wash and pat dry. Brown in remaining oil. Add to the soup, cover and simmer for another 45 minutes longer.

3. Remove all the stew ingredients with a slotted spoon, reserving juice. Mash meat and eggplant with a wooden mortar and pestle or in a food processor.

4. Return puree to broth and cook 15 minutes over low heat, stirring constantly. Add *kashke* or sour cream and stir thoroughly for about 5 minutes. Remove from heat. If you are using *kashke*, reduce amount of salt to 1 teaspoon.

5. Taste and correct seasoning. Place puree in a serving bowl.

6. For the garnish, heat 2 tablespoons oil in a skillet and brown the onion and garlic. Remove from heat and add mint. Decorate the puree with this mixture, pieces of walnut and a dollop of *kashke* or sour cream and the saffron. Serve with bread.

Note: *Kashke* or liquid whey is available at some food specialty stores (page 240). Since it is not always of good quality, I prefer to use sour cream.

Eggplant with Sour Cream or Kashke

Makes 4 servings
Preparation time: 50 min.
Cooking time: 40 min.

3 medium eggplants
2 large onions, chopped
½ pound stew lamb, veal or beef, cut in ½-inch cubes
½ cup butter or oil
2 tablespoons yellow split peas
½ tablespoon tomato paste
½ teaspoon salt
¼ teaspoon freshly ground black pepper
1 cup water

GARNISH
2 cloves garlic, crushed (optional)
1 tablespoon oil
1 tablespoon dried mint
1½ cups *kashke* (liquid whey) or sour cream
¼ teaspoon saffron dissolved in 1 tablespoon hot water
3–4 quartered walnuts
2–3 pitted dates

Kashk-e Bademjan

1. Peel and cut eggplants in lengthwise slices. Sprinkle with 1 teaspoon salt. Let stand for 20 minutes. Wash and dry with a towel.

2. In a saucepan, brown 1 onion and meat in 3 tablespoons oil. Add split peas, tomato paste, ½ teaspoon salt, ¼ teaspoon pepper and 1 cup water. Cover and cook approximately 30 minutes over low heat.

3. Heat 3 tablespoons of oil in a skillet and brown eggplant on all sides, adding more oil if necessary.

4. Saute remaining onion in 2 tablespoons oil and set aside.

5. Arrange layers of eggplant and layers of sauteed onions in a long ovenproof dish and top with mixture of meat and split peas. Cover and bake in preheated 350°F oven for about 40 minutes.

6. Just before serving, brown crushed garlic cloves in a little oil. Remove skillet from heat and add dried mint powder.

7. Remove baking dish from oven. Pour 1 cup *kashke* or sour cream on top. Garnish with sauteed garlic and mint, diluted saffron, walnut pieces and pitted dates. Serve with bread and chopped herbs.

Note: *Kashke* or liquid whey is available in food specialty shops (page 240). Since it is not always of good quality, I prefer to use sour cream or yogurt.

Wheat Puree

Makes 6 servings
Preparation time: 15 min. plus 1
hr. soaking time
Cooking time: 2 hrs. 30 min.

1 **pound boned shoulder of**
lamb, veal or beef, left whole
2 **onions, finely chopped**
1 **cup chick-peas (optional)**
1½ **teaspoons salt**
1 **pound whole wheat berries,**
soaked for 1 hour in 2 cups
water

GARNISH
¼ **cup butter**
1 **teaspoon cinnamon**
2 **teaspoons confectioners sugar**

Halim-e Gandom

1. Place the piece of meat in a large pot. Add onion, chick-peas, 6 cups water and 1½ teaspoons salt. Bring to a boil, skimming the froth as it forms. Cover and simmer over low heat for 1 hour, adding warm water if needed. Stir occasionally to prevent sticking to the bottom.

2. Add pre-soaked whole wheat berries to the pot. Cover and simmer for 1 hour over low heat, adding more water if necessary.

3. Check to see that stew ingredients are done. Remove with a slotted spoon, reserving juice. Mash with mortar and pestle or in a food processor.

4. Return to pot and combine with meat broth. Cook, stirring constantly for 15 minutes over low heat, until the mixture reaches the consistency of a smooth porridge.

5. Place in a serving bowl. Garnish with ¼ cup melted butter, cinnamon and sugar.

Variation: This dish may also be prepared using 2 cups of Cream of Wheat cereal dissolved in 3 cups milk in place of the soaked whole wheat berries.

E G G D I S H E S

The Smell of a Thought

Mulla Nasrudin was penniless and sat huddled in a blanket while the wind howled outside. "At least," he thought, "the people next door will not smell cooking from my kitchen–so they can't send round to cadge some food."

At that the thought of hot, aromatic soup came into his mind, and he savored it mentally for several minutes. There came a knocking on the door.

"Mother sent me," said the little daughter of his neighbor, "to ask whether you had any soup to spare, hot, seasoned soup."

"Heaven help us," said Mulla, "the neighbors even smell my thoughts."

E g g   D i s h e s

Eggs and egg dishes are popular throughout the Middle East. Iranians are especially fond of *kookoo,* a type of omelet similar to the Italian *frittata* and the Arab *eggah*. It is filled with meat, vegetables or herbs. A good *kookoo* is thick and rather fluffy.

Although nowadays this dish is usually prepared in the oven, traditionally it was cooked in a large covered skillet that was set on hot coals. Coals were placed on the cover as well.

Kookoos are served as appetizers, side dishes or as a main dish with yogurt or salad and bread. They may be eaten hot or cold and they keep well in the refrigerator for two or three days.

Most Iranian households keep *kookoos* on hand for snacks or to serve unexpected guests. They are ideal for picnics as well.

Eggplant Kookoo

Makes 4 servings
Preparation time: 30 min.
Cooking time: 45 min.

كوكو بادمجان

Kookoo-ye Bademjan

2 large eggplants, about 2 pounds
⅔ cup oil
2 onions, thinly sliced
2 cloves garlic, crushed
6 eggs
Juice of 1 lemon
1 teaspoon salt

¼ teaspoon freshly ground pepper
¼ teaspoon saffron, dissolved in 1 tablespoon hot water

1. Peel eggplants and slice lengthwise. Sprinkle with salt and drain in colander for 20 minutes. Wash and pat dry.

2. In a skillet, brown eggplant slices in ½ cup oil. Remove from skillet, cool and mash with a fork.

3. In same skillet, brown onions and garlic in remaining oil.

4. Break eggs into a bowl. Add lemon juice, salt and pepper and saffron. Beat thoroughly with a fork.

5. Add mashed eggplants, onions and garlic to beaten egg mixture. Taste and adjust seasoning.

6. Pour remaining oil into a 9-inch ovenproof dish or mold and place in pre-heated 350°F oven. When the oil is hot, remove dish and pour in egg mixture. Return to oven immediately and bake uncovered for 45 minutes.

7. Serve the *kookoo* in the baking dish or unmold it by loosening the edges with the tip of a knife and inverting it onto a serving platter.

8. Serve with yogurt, bread and a dish of raw vegetables and fresh herbs.

Variation: Zucchini may be substituted for eggplant.

Note: The kookoo can also be cooked on top of the stove. Heat the oil in a skillet, pour in the mixture, then cook, covered, over low heat until it has set, about 15 minutes. Turn kookoo over by cutting it into pieces and turning them over one by one. Or pass the kookoo under the broiler just long enough to brown the top lightly.

Cauliflower Kookoo

Makes 4 servings
Preparation time: 35 min.
Cooking time: 45 min.

1 small head cauliflower or half a large head
1 onion, chopped
⅓ cup oil or butter
6 eggs
¼ teaspoon saffron, dissolved in 1 tablespoon hot water
1½ teaspoons salt
¼ teaspoon freshly ground black pepper
1 teaspoon baking soda

Kookoo-ye Gol-e Kalam

1. Wash cauliflower and break into flowerets; cook in saucepan for 15 minutes over medium heat in 2 cups water and ¼ teaspoon salt. Drain and mash. Allow to cool.

2. In a skillet, brown onion in 3 tablespoons oil or butter.

3. Break eggs into a bowl. Add saffron, salt, pepper and baking soda. Beat thoroughly with a fork.

4. Add mashed cauliflower and onion to beaten eggs. Mix, taste and adjust seasoning.

5. Pour remaining oil into an ovenproof dish or mold and place in preheated 350°F oven. When oil is hot, remove dish from oven. Pour in the egg mixture. Return dish to oven and bake uncovered about 45 minutes or until it is golden brown on top.

6. Serve the cauliflower *kookoo* in the baking dish or unmold it by loosening the edges with the tip of a knife and inverting it onto a serving platter. Serve with fresh herbs, *torshi* (page 164) or yogurt (page 212).

Note: *Kookoo* can also be cooked on top of the stove. Heat the oil or butter in a skillet, pour in the mixture, then cook, covered, over low heat until it has set, about 15 minutes. Turn the *kookoo* over by cutting it into wedges and turning them over one by one. Or pass the *kookoo* under the broiler just long enough to brown the top lightly.

Green Bean Kookoo

Makes 4 servings
Preparation time: 25 min.
Cooking time: 45 min.

کوکوی لوبیاسبز

Kookoo-ye Loubia
Sabz

1 pound fresh or frozen green
  beans, cut into 1-inch pieces
2 medium onions, chopped
2 cloves garlic, crushed
⅓ cup oil or butter
6 eggs
1 tablespoon flour
¼ teaspoon baking soda
¼ teaspoon saffron, dissolved in
  1 tablespoon hot water

1 tablespoon lemon juice
1 teaspoon salt
¼ teaspoon pepper

1. Place green beans in a saucepan with 2 cups water and ¼ teaspoon salt; cover and cook for 15 minutes over medium heat. Drain and cool.

2. In a skillet, brown onions and garlic in 3 tablespoons oil or butter. Remove from heat and set aside.

3. Break eggs in a bowl. Add flour, baking soda, saffron, lemon juice, 1 teaspoon salt and ¼ teaspoon pepper. Beat thoroughly with a fork.

4. Add drained green beans and onions to beaten eggs. Mix and taste for seasoning.

5. Pour remaining oil into a 9-inch ovenproof dish or mold and place in pre-heated 350°F oven. When oil is hot, remove dish and pour in egg and bean mixture. Return dish to oven and bake uncovered for 45 minutes.

6. Serve the *kookoo* in the baking dish or unmold it by loosening edges with point of a knife and inverting it onto a serving platter.

Note: *Kookoo* can also be cooked on top of the stove. Heat the oil or butter in a skillet, pour in the mixture, then cook, covered, over low heat until it has set, about 15 minutes. Turn the *kookoo* over by cutting it into wedges and turning them over one by one. Or pass the *kookoo* under the broiler just long enough to brown the top lightly.

Bread and Cheese with Fresh Vegetables and Herbs
Nan-o Panir-o Sabzi-Khordan
page 8

Stuffed Green Peppers, Eggplants and Tomatoes
Dolmeh-e Felfel Sabz-o Bademjan-o Gojeh Farangi
page 44

Vinegar Syrup with Lettuce
Sharbat-e Sekanjebine ba Kahou
page 229

Plum Paste Rolls
Lavashak
page 179

Green Pea Kookoo

Makes 4 servings
Preparation time: 10 min.
Cooking time: 1 hr.

2 cups green peas, fresh or frozen
1 onion, chopped
2 cloves garlic, crushed
¼ cup oil or butter
6 eggs
1 cup chopped fresh dill or ½ cup dried dill weed
1 teaspoon salt

¼ teaspoon freshly ground black pepper
¼ teaspoon saffron, dissolved in 1 tablespoon hot water
¼ teaspoon baking soda

Kookoo-ye Nokhod Sabz

1. Boil the peas in 1 cup water until tender, about 10 minutes. Drain and allow to cool.

2. Brown the onion and garlic in 1 tablespoon oil.

3. Beat the eggs in a bowl, add all the other ingredients and mix well.

4. Pour the remaining oil in a 9-inch ovenproof baking dish or mold and place in preheated 350°F oven. When hot, pour the egg and pea mixture in and bake uncovered for 45 to 60 minutes.

5. The *kookoo* may be served directly from the dish or unmolded onto a serving platter. Serve with bread, yogurt (page 212) and fresh herbs.

Note: Pea *kookoo* can also be cooked on top of the stove. Heat the oil or butter in a skillet, pour in the mixture, then cook, covered, over low heat until it has set, about 15 minutes. Turn the *kookoo* over by cutting it into wedges and turning them over one by one. Or pass the *kookoo* under the broiler just long enough to brown the top lightly.

Potato Kookoo

Makes 4 servings
Preparation time: 30 min.
Cooking time: 25 min.

1 pound potatoes
3 eggs
¼ teaspoon ground saffron
  dissolved in 1 tablespoon hot
  water
1 onion, grated
½ teaspoon salt
3 tablespoons oil or butter
3 tablespoons confectioners
  sugar for garnish

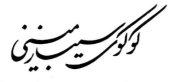

Kookoo-ye Sibzamini

1. Boil potatoes in 2 cups salted water for 30 minutes. Peel and mash them. Allow to cool.

2. Break eggs into a bowl. Add saffron, grated onion and salt. Beat well with a fork.

3. Add mashed potatoes to eggs and mix well.

4. Pour oil or butter into a 9-inch ovenproof dish or mold and place in pre-heated 350°F oven. When oil is hot, pour in egg and potato mixture. Bake uncovered for 25 minutes.

5. Serve potato *kookoo* in the dish or unmold it by loosening the edges with the tip of a knife and inverting it onto a serving platter. Serve with bread, yogurt (page 212) and fresh herbs or sprinkle with powdered sugar.

Note: The egg and potato mixture can also be shaped into patties 3 inches in diameter by scooping a ladleful of batter and pouring it into a skillet. Fry in oil on both sides until golden brown.

Herb Kookoo

Makes 4 servings
Preparation time: 20 min.
Cooking time: 45 min.

8 eggs
½ teaspoon baking soda
1 teaspoon flour
1 tablespoon barberries (optional)
⅓ cup coarsely chopped walnuts (optional)
1 teaspoon salt
¼ teaspoon freshly ground black pepper
¼ cup oil or butter

½ cup chopped chives or scallions
1 cup chopped parsley
¼ cup chopped fresh coriander leaves or 2 tablespoons dried
½ cup chopped fresh dill
3 leaves of lettuce, chopped

Kookoo-ye Sabzi

Herb kookoo is a traditional New Year's dish in Iran. Green in color, it symbolizes fruitfulness, and eating herb kookoo is believed to bring prosperity and happiness in the year to come.

1. Break eggs into a bowl. Add baking soda, flour, barberries, walnuts, salt, pepper and 2 tablespoons oil. Beat well with a fork. Add chopped herbs and greens, mix thoroughly and correct seasoning.

2. Pour remaining oil into an ovenproof dish or mold and place in preheated 350°F oven. When the oil is hot, pour in the egg mixture. Bake uncovered for 45 minutes.

3. Present the *kookoo* in the baking dish or unmold it onto a serving platter. Serve it hot or cold, cut into small pieces, with bread and yogurt (page 212).

Variation: Herb *kookoo* may also be cooked on top of the. Heat the oil or butter in a skillet, pour in the mixture, then cook, covered, over low heat until it has set, about 15 minutes. Turn the *kookoo* over by cutting it into wedges and turning them over one by one. Or pass the *kookoo* under the broiler just long enough to brown the top lightly.

Note: Dried barberries are available at Middle Eastern food shops (page 240). They should be soaked for 10 minutes in cold water, rinsed and drained before being added to the mixture.

Chicken Kookoo

Makes 6 servings
Preparation times: 1 hr.
Cooking time: 25 min.

1 small chicken, about 2½ pounds, cut up (leftover chicken or turkey may be used instead)
2 onions, chopped
⅓ cup oil
6 eggs
¼ teaspoon saffron dissolved in 1 tablespoon hot water
½ teaspoon baking soda

1 tablespoon lemon juice
1 teaspoon salt
¼ teaspoon freshly ground black pepper

Kookoo-ye Joojeh

1. Place the chicken in a saucepan with 1 onion, cover and simmer for 45 minutes over low heat. It is not necessary to add water; chicken and onion will produce enough juice. Remove chicken, debone it, cut into small pieces and set aside to cool.

2. In a skillet, brown other onion in 3 tablespoons oil.

3. Break eggs into a bowl. Add browned onion, saffron, baking soda, lemon juice, salt and pepper. Beat the mixture thoroughly with a fork.

4. Add chicken pieces to beaten eggs. Mix thoroughly, taste and correct seasoning.

5. Pour remaining oil into a 9-inch ovenproof dish or mold and place in preheated 350°F oven. When oil is hot, pour in egg mixture. Return dish to oven immediately and bake uncovered for 25 minutes.

6. Present the *kookoo* in the dish or unmold it onto a serving platter. Serve with fresh vegetables and herbs (*sabzi-khordan*, page 8), Persian pickles (*torshi*, page 164) or yogurt (page 212).

Note: Chicken *kookoo* can also be cooked on top of the stove. Heat the oil or butter in a skillet, pour in the mixture, then cook, covered, over low heat until it has set, about 15 minutes. Turn the *kookoo* over by cutting it into wedges and turning them over one by one. Or pass the *kookoo* under the broiler just long enough to brown the top lightly.

Meat Kookoo

Makes 4 servings
Preparation time: 20 min.
Cooking time: 30 min.

2 onions, chopped
1 pound ground beef
⅓ cup oil or butter
1 cup chopped parsley
½ cup chopped chives or scallions
1¼ teaspoons salt
¼ teaspoon freshly ground black pepper

6 eggs
¼ teaspoon cinnamon
1 teaspoon curry powder

Kookoo-ye Gusht

1. In a skillet, brown onions and meat in 3 tablespoons oil. Add chopped parsley and chives or scallions, 1 teaspoon salt and ¼ teaspoon pepper. Stir well.

2. Break eggs into a bowl. Add cinnamon, curry powder, ¼ teaspoon salt and a pinch of pepper. Beat the mixture thoroughly with a fork.

3. Add meat to eggs. Mix thoroughly, taste and correct seasoning.

4. Pour remaining oil into a 9-inch ovenproof dish or mold and place in pre-heated 350°F oven. When oil is hot, pour in egg and meat mixture. Place in oven and bake uncovered for 30 minutes.

5. Present the *kookoo* in the baking dish or unmold it and invert it onto a serving plate. Serve with bread, fresh herbs, yogurt (page 212) or *torshi* (page 164).

Variation: The parsley and chives can be replaced with 5 medium eggplants, peeled and cut into ½-inch cubes and browned in oil.

Note: Meat kookoo *can also be cooked on top of the stove. Heat the oil or butter in a skillet, pour in the mixture, then cook, covered, over low heat until it has set, about 15 minutes. Turn the* kookoo *over by cutting it into wedges and turning them over one by one. Or pass the* kookoo *under the broiler just long enough to brown the top lightly.*

Brain Kookoo

Makes 4 servings
Preparation time: 15 min.
Cooking time: 30 min.

2 lamb brains or 1 calf's brain
5 eggs
1 teaspoon salt
¼ teaspoon freshly ground black pepper
¼ teaspoon saffron, dissolved in 1 tablespoon hot water

2 cloves garlic, crushed
½ cup chopped parsley
½ cup oil or butter

Kookoo-ye Maghz

1. Drop brains into boiling water and cook for 10 minutes. Drain and remove the membranes.

2. Mash the brain thoroughly in a food processor.

3. Beat the eggs in a bowl, add salt, pepper, saffron, garlic and parsley and mix well.

4. Pour the oil into a 9-inch ovenproof dish and place in preheated 350°F oven. When the oil is hot, pour in the egg mixture, return dish to oven immediately and bake uncovered for 30 minutes.

5. Serve the *kookoo* in the dish or unmolded onto a platter with bread and fresh herbs.

Note: Brain *kookoo* can also be cooked on top of the stove. Heat the oil or butter in a skillet, pour in the mixture, then cook, covered, over low heat until it has set, about 15 minutes. Turn the *kookoo* over by cutting it into wedges and turning them over one by one. Or pass the *kookoo* under the broiler just long enough to brown the top lightly.

Fish Kookoo

Makes 4 to 6 servings
Preparation time: 40 min.
Cooking time: 30 min.

1 pound fillet of sole or fillet of flounder
½ cup butter
1 onion, grated
2 cloves garlic, crushed
4 eggs, beaten
1 tablespoon flour
½ teaspoon baking soda
¼ cup chopped parsley

1 tablespoon lemon juice
1 teaspoon salt
¼ teaspoon freshly ground black pepper

Kookoo-ye Mahi

1. Wash and dry the fish and sprinkle with flour and salt to prevent fish from sticking to the pan. Heat 3 tablespoons butter in a skillet and saute fish until brown on both sides. Cool and remove any bones. Chop fine.

2. Preheat oven to 350°F.

3. Saute onion and garlic in 1 tablespoon butter.

4. In a bowl, beat the eggs, add 1 tablespoon flour, baking soda, parsley, onion, garlic, lemon juice, 1 teaspoon salt and ¼ teaspoon pepper and beat well. Mix in fish.

5. Grease a 9-inch ovenproof dish with 2 tablespoons melted butter. Pour in the fish and egg mixture and spread evenly. Pour remaining butter evenly over the top. Bake uncovered in oven at 350°F for 30 minutes or until set.

6. Serve the *kookoo* in the baking dish or unmold it by loosening the edges with the tip of a knife and inverting it onto a serving platter.

7. Serve with lemon juice and bread.

Note: Fish *kookoo* can also be cooked on top of the stove. Heat the oil or butter in a skillet, pour in the mixture, cover, then cook over low heat until it has set, about 15 minutes. Turn the *kookoo* over by cutting it into wedges and turning them over one by one. Or pass the *kookoo* under the broiler just long enough to brown the top lightly.

Yogurt Kookoo

Makes 4 servings
Preparation time: 10 min.
Cooking time: 20 min.

4 **eggs**
1 **teaspoon flour**
¼ **teaspoon saffron, dissolved in 1 tablespoon hot water**
½ **teaspoon salt**
¼ **teaspoon freshly ground black pepper**
½ **cup chopped chives or scallions**
1 **large carrot, grated**

½ **cup yogurt**
1 **teaspoon slivered almonds**
4 **tablespoons oil**

Kookoo-ye Mast

1. Break eggs into a bowl. Add flour, saffron, salt and pepper, chives and carrot. Beat thoroughly with a fork.

2. Add yogurt and slivered almonds to egg mixture. Mix well and taste for seasoning.

3. Pour oil into an ovenproof dish or mold and place in preheated 350°F oven. When oil is hot, pour in egg mixture and return to oven and bake uncovered for 20 minutes.

4. Serve the *kookoo* in the dish or unmold it by loosening the edges with the tip of a knife and inverting it onto a serving platter.

Note: Yogurt *kookoo* can also be cooked on top of the stove. Heat the oil or butter in a skillet, pour in the mixture, then cook, covered, over low heat until it has set, about 15 minutes. Turn the *kookoo* over by cutting it into wedges and turning them over one by one. Or pass the *kookoo* under the broiler just long enough to brown the top lightly.

Eggplant Omelet

Makes 4 servings
Preparation time: 30 min.
Cooking time: 15 min.

2 small eggplants
½ cup oil
3 cloves garlic, crushed
1 large onion, finely sliced
1 large tomato, peeled and chopped
¼ teaspoon turmeric

2 eggs
½ teaspoon salt
¼ teaspoon freshly ground black pepper

Mirza Ghasemi

1. Preheat oven to 400°F. Prick eggplants with a fork to prevent bursting and place on oven rack. Bake for 30 minutes.

2. Remove from oven, peel and chop.

3. Heat the oil in a skillet and saute the garlic, onion, eggplants and tomato. Add the turmeric. Cook over medium heat for 10 minutes.

4. Break eggs into a bowl; add salt and pepper. Beat well with a fork.

5. Pour into skillet and cook over low heat until eggs are firm, stirring occasionally with a wooden spoon.

6. Transfer to a serving platter. Serve with bread, fresh herbs and yogurt (page 212).

Eggs on Spinach

Makes 3 servings
Preparation time: 10 min.
Cooking time: 10 min.

2 cups fresh or frozen chopped
   spinach
1 onion, sliced thin
3 tablespoons oil or butter
1 clove garlic, crushed
¼ teaspoon salt
¼ teaspoon freshly ground black
   pepper
3 eggs

Nargesi-ye Esfenaj

1. Steam spinach in a steamer for 10 minutes and set aside.

2. Brown onion in oil; add garlic and cook briefly. Stir in spinach and season with salt and pepper. Mix well and cook over medium heat for 3 minutes. Spread out the mixture evenly in the skillet.

3. Break eggs over layer of spinach, cover and cook over very low heat for 3 to 5 minutes or until eggs have set.

4. Transfer to serving platter and serve immediately.

Nargesi is the Persian word for narcissus, a flower with white petals and a bright yellow center. To the fanciful, the colors of a dish of eggs poached on a bed of green suggest that flower of early springtime.

MEAT, CHICKEN AND FISH

گر دست دهد ز مغز گندم نانی

و ز می دو منی ز گوسفند رانی

با لاله رخی نشسته در بستانی

عیشی بود این نه حد هر سلطانی

If one may have a loaf of the flower of wheat, a two-
  Maund jar of wine, a thigh of mutton, seated with
A heart's darling in a ruined place—that is a pleasure
That is not the attainment of any sultan.

Omar Khayyam

M e a t s

Mutton or lamb is the meat used most in Persian cooking. All the parts of the sheep are used, not only the prime cuts of the leg, shoulder and loin, but also the feet and the head as well as all the organs, such as lamb fries, known in America as Rocky Mountain oysters (the testicles).

Lamb brochettes (*kabab*), convenient and virtually foolproof, are very popular. The meat is left to marinate in herbs and vinegar or lemon or yogurt. Then, when it is nearly time to eat, the meat is threaded on skewers and cooked over charcoal for a subtly perfumed, flame-rich flavor. We like to use the very tender meat from the loin, but leg of lamb can also be used as long as it is marinated for at least 24 hours before grilling.

Ground meat brochettes are also easy to make and bound to please. The meat is mixed with onions and spices and molded on flat swordlike skewers. Then it is cooked just long enough to be seared on the outside, pink and juicy within.

Such dishes can be broiled indoors in the stove but the flavor will not be as haunting as when the meat is imbued with the odor of a charcoal flame.

Whole Stuffed Baby Lamb

*Makes 12 servings
Preparation time: 1 hr. 30 min.
Cooking time: 3 to 4 hrs.*

بره درسته توپر

*Bareh-e Dorosteh
Tu Por*

This spectacular dish is served on festive occasions. It is often the centerpiece of a lavish Persian wedding feast. Several lambs would be prepared to serve all the guests.

1 baby lamb, 14–18 pounds
Juice of 2 onions
1 teaspoon salt
10 cloves garlic
2 teaspoons ground saffron, dissolved in ¼ cup hot water
½ cup melted butter

STUFFING
3 cups long-grain rice
2 teaspoons salt
4 large onions, chopped
2 cloves garlic, chopped
  Liver, heart and kidneys of lamb, washed and chopped
½ cup butter
1 cup scallions, chopped
1 cup parsley, chopped
¼ cup tarragon, chopped
1 cup corriander, chopped
1 cup almonds, chopped
½ cup pistachio nuts, chopped
2 cups raisins
2 cups walnuts, chopped
2 cups apricots, chopped
2 cups dried barberries, cleaned and soaked for 10 minutes in water and drained
2 cups pitted dates, chopped
4 apples, peeled, cored and chopped
2 teaspoons turmeric
1 teaspoon black pepper

1. Order your lamb ahead of time. Ask the butcher to prepare the lamb and bone the legs.

2. Rinse the lamb inside and out, and wipe dry with a towel.

3. Rub inside and out with mixture of onion juice and 1 teaspoon salt.

4. Using the point of a small knife, make 10 slits in the lamb and insert a clove of garlic in each. Set aside while preparing the stuffing.

5. In a saucepan, cook rice 20 minutes in 9 cups water and 2 tablespoons salt. Drain and set aside.

6. In a large skillet, saute the onions, garlic, liver, heart and kidneys in ½ cup butter. Add the scallions, parsley, tarragon, corriander, almonds, pistachios, raisins, walnuts, apricots, barberries, dates, apples, turmeric, 2 teaspoons salt and the pepper. Cook for 5 minutes.

7. In a large bowl, combine all the stuffing ingredients with rice and mix well.

8. Stuff the lamb tightly with this mixture and sew the belly using a large trussing needle and strong kitchen thread.

9. Place lamb in a roasting pan in a preheated 350°F oven and cook for about 4 hours or until meat separates easily from the bone. Using a pastry brush, baste the lamb occasionally with a mixture of saffron and melted butter and the pan juice.

10. Arrange lamb on an oval platter in the center of a huge mound of rice with saffron (*chelo*, page 95).

11. Serve with *torshi* (page 164) and *sabzi-khordan* (fresh vegetables and herbs).

Note: As an alternative, you may wrap the lamb in foil and roast it in a preheated 375°F oven, uncovering it for the last ½ hour of cooking. Roast about 2 hours for a well-done lamb and 1½ hours for rare.

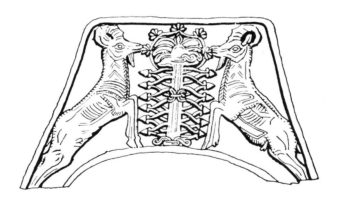

Lamb Stew

Makes 6 Servings
Preparation time: 15 min.
Cooking time: 2 hrs.

2 pounds lean shoulder of lamb, veal or roast beef, boned and sliced
3 large onions, sliced
3 tomatoes, peeled and sliced
1 quince or if not available, 2 apples
4 tablespoons oil
2 cloves garlic, crushed
1 small eggplant, peeled and sliced
2 carrots, peeled and sliced
2 large potatoes, peeled and sliced
1 cup pitted prunes

1 teaspoon *advieh* (allspice, page 160)
¼ teaspoon turmeric
2 teaspoons salt
¼ teaspoon freshly ground pepper
1 tablespoon tomato paste dissolved in 2 tablespoons hot water
¼ teaspoon saffron, dissolved in 1 tablespoon hot water
1 tablespoon powdered *limou-omani* (dried Persian limes)

Tas Kabab

1. Slice meat, onions and tomatoes. Wash, core and slice quince or apple.

2. Pour 2 tablespoons oil into a large heavy Dutch oven. Layer the ingredients in the following order: onions, meat, garlic, quince or apple, eggplants, carrots, tomatoes and potatoes. Top with a layer of prunes. Pour in the remaining oil. Sprinkle allspice, turmeric, salt and pepper on top. Stir in the dissolved tomato paste, saffron and *limou-omani*, cover and cook for 2 hours or more over low heat until done. Correct seasoning.

3. Arrange on a platter and serve piping hot.

Variation: This stew may also be cooked in a preheated 350°F oven. Place ingredients in an ovenproof dish, cover and cook for 45 minutes. Uncover, add tomato paste and bake for another 45 minutes.

Note: Limou-omani *(dried Persian limes) and* advieh *are available at Middle Eastern food specialty shops (page 240).*

Lamb Brochettes

Makes 6 servings
Preparation time: 20 min. plus 24 hrs. marinating
Cooking time: 10 min.

2 pounds boned loin or leg of lamb, beef or veal
3 large onions, chopped
2 cloves garlic, crushed
¼ teaspoon ground saffron, dissolved in 2 tablespoons water
1 cup yogurt
2 tablespoons butter

Juice of 1 lemon
1 teaspoon salt
8 small tomatoes

Kabab-e Barg

1. Cut meat into 2-inch cubes and pound each piece of meat with a small mallet. Place in a large bowl.

2. Add onions, garlic, half the saffron and yogurt. Mix well. Cover and marinate for at least 24 hours in refrigerator.

3. Start a bed of charcoal at least 30 minutes before cooking and let it burn until evenly lit.

4. During this time, spear 5 to 6 pieces of meat on each skewer, leaving ends free. Spear tomatoes on separate skewers.

5. In a small saucepan, melt butter. Add lemon juice, remaining saffron and salt. Set aside in a warm place.

6. When the coals are ready, place tomatoes on grill; after 3 minutes, place meat brochettes on the grill. Cook for 3 to 4 minutes on either side. The meat should be seared on the outside, pink and juicy on the inside.

7. When the brochettes are cooked, brush them with the butter mixture. Arrange brochettes on a serving platter. Remove meat from skewers using a piece of bread. Garnish with grilled tomatoes. Cover with a piece of bread to keep everything warm.

8. Serve immediately with *chelo* (page 95), pita bread or *torshi* (page 164) and a dish of raw vegetables and fresh herbs.

Lamb Brochettes with Vegetables

Makes 4 servings
Preparation time: 20 min. plus 24 hrs. marinating
Cooking time: 10 min.

2 **pounds lamb from the boned loin or leg or beef or veal, cut in 2-inch cubes**
1 **large onion, grated**
⅔ **cup vinegar**
1 **clove garlic, crushed**
1 **teaspoon dried oregano**
4 **green peppers**
6 **large tomatoes, quartered, or 2 pounds cherry tomatoes left whole**

10 **small onions or 3 large ones cut in 2-inch cubes**
2 **tablespoons butter**
  Juice of 1 lemon
½ **teaspoon salt**

Shish Kabab

1. Pound each piece of meat with a small mallet and place in a large bowl. Add grated onion, vinegar, garlic and oregano. Mix well. Cover and marinate for at least 24 hours in refrigerator.

2. Start charcoal at least 30 minutes before cooking and let it burn until evenly lit.

3. Remove seeds from peppers and cut into 2-inch squares.

4. Spear meat on skewers, alternating with pieces of pepper, tomato and onions.

5. When the coals are evenly lit with white ash around each coal and the grill very hot, place brochettes on grill rack. Grill for 3-5 minutes on either side.

6. In a saucepan, melt the butter, add lemon juice and ½ teaspoon salt, and brush over skewered meat and vegetables. The meat should be seared on the outside, pink and juicy on the inside.

7. Arrange brochettes on a serving platter. Serve immediately with *chelo* (page 95) or bread.

Liver, Heart and Kidney Brochettes

Makes 4 servings
Preparation time: 20 min.
Cooking time: 6 min.

Kabab-e Jigar-o
Del-o-Gholveh

1 lamb's liver or ½ pound piece calf's liver
4 lamb kidneys or 1 veal kidney
4 lamb hearts or ¼ of a calf's heart
½ teaspoon salt

¼ teaspoon freshly ground black pepper
Juice of 3 limes

1. Clean liver and cut into strips 1-inch thick. Cut kidneys into 1-inch cubes and slice hearts lengthwise into strips 1½ inches thick.

2. Light a bed of charcoal and let it burn until evenly lit, or heat the broiler in your oven.

3. Thread slices of liver, pieces of kidney and slices of heart onto separate skewers (cooking times are different for each).

4. Grill over hot coals for approximately 6 minutes for heart, 5 for kidney and 4 for the liver brochettes, turning frequently.

5. After cooking, sprinkle with salt, pepper and lime juice.

6. Serve immediately with bread, scallions and *torshi* (page 164), or use as an appetizer with drinks.

Variation: A marvelous way to cook these brochettes while sitting around the fire is to place a special cooking grill inside your fireplace.

Broiled Lamb Fries

4 lamb fries
2 tablespoons melted butter

Makes 4 servings
Preparation time: 10 min.
Cooking time: 6 min.

Kabab-e Donbalan

1. Place the lamb fries in a large bowl of cool water; wash and drain them and cut each one in half.

2. Remove the thin outer membranes from the fries.

3. Light a bed of charcoal and let it burn until evenly lit, or heat the broiler in your oven.

4. Thread the fries on skewers. Paint them with melted butter and grill them over the hot coals for about 4–6 minutes, turning often and quickly.

5. Serve very hot and season to taste with salt and pepper.

Wherever lamb is raised for meat, the fries or testicles are considered a great delicacy. They are usually referred to by euphemism, such as Rocky Mountain or prairie oysters or swinging steak in the United States, or caprices de femme (lady's whims) in France. Whatever you call them, they are excellent as an appetizer served with drinks.

Chicken Brochettes

Makes 4 servings
Preparation time: 20 min. plus 6 hrs. marinating
Cooking time: 15 min.

2 broiling chickens, about 2 pounds each
¼ teaspoon saffron, dissolved in 1 tablespoon water
1 cup lemon juice
2 large onions, chopped
2 teaspoons salt
¼ cup butter

Juice of 1 lemon
Limes for garnish
Parsley sprigs for garnish

Joojeh Kabab

1. Cut each chicken into 10 pieces.

2. Wash and pat dry pieces of chicken.

3. In a large bowl, combine half the saffron and 1 cup lemon juice, the onions and 2 teaspoons salt. Beat well with a fork. Add the pieces of chicken and baste with marinade. Mix well, cover and marinate at least 6 hours and up to 2 days in refrigerator.

4. Start a bed of charcoal at least 30 minutes before cooking. Let it burn until the coals are evenly lit, or heat the oven broiler.

5. Spear wings, breasts and legs on separate skewers because they require different cooking times.

6. Melt butter in small saucepan. Add juice of 1 fresh lemon and remaining saffron.

7. Grill brochettes for 8 to 15 minutes, putting the legs on first, then the breasts and wings. Turn occasionally. When cooked, paint with butter mixture. The chicken is done when the juice that runs out is yellow rather than pink.

8. Remove broiled chicken from skewers. Arrange on serving platter. Garnish with limes cut in half and sprigs of parsley.

9. Serve immediately with bread, fresh herbs and *torshi* (page 164) or french fries.

Note: You may grill the chicken pieces in a broiling pan in a broiler for 10 minutes on each side. During the grilling the door of the broiler should be closed. This way the broiled chicken will be tender. There is no need to spear chicken pieces on skewers.

Stuffed Chicken

Makes 4 servings
Preparation time: 35 min.
Cooking time: 2 hrs. 25 min.

1 large roasting chicken with giblets, about 6 to 7 pounds, or 2 small fryer chickens
2 teaspoons salt
2 large onions, finely sliced
2 cloves garlic, crushed
½ cup rice, cleaned and washed
2 tablespoons slivered almonds
2 tablespoons raisins
2 tablespoons dried barberries, soaked for 10 minutes and drained

½ tablespoon *advieh* (allspice, page 160)
¼ teaspoon freshly ground black pepper
½ cup chicken stock
¼ teaspoon saffron, dissolved in 1 tablespoon hot water
½ cup melted butter
Lemon slices for garnish

Morgh-e Tu Por

1. Clean and wash chicken and rub with 1 teaspoon salt.

2. Brown onions and garlic in a skillet; add rice, almonds, raisins, barberries, allspice, 1 teaspoon salt, ¼ teaspoon pepper and chicken giblets. Cook 5 minutes, stirring occasionally.

3. Add chicken stock; cover and simmer over low heat for 20 minutes.

4. Stuff chicken with this mixture and pin or sew shut cavity.

5. Paint chicken with mixture of saffron and melted butter. Place in an oven-proof dish or roasting pan and cover with aluminum foil.

6. Place in preheated 350°F and roast for 2 hours, basting occasionally with butter and saffron sauce or the pan juices.

7. When the chicken is done, serve in the ovenproof dish or on a serving platter. Garnish with lemon slices.

8. Serve with bread, raw vegetables and fresh herbs and salad.

Note: If dried barberries are used, they must be soaked in a bowl of cold water for 10 minutes first. Lift out carefully, rinse and drain. Dried barberries and *advieh* are available in Middle Eastern food specialty shops (page 240).

Sweet and Sour Stuffed Chicken

Makes 4 servings
Preparation time: 30 min.
Cooking time: 2 hrs.

1	large roasting chicken, with giblets, 6–7 pounds, or 2 small fryer chickens
2½	teaspoons salt
1	tablespoon oil
1	large onion, chopped
2	cloves garlic, crushed
1	cup prunes, pitted and finely chopped
1	apple, cored and chopped
1	cup dried apricots, finely chopped

½	cup raisins
¼	teaspoon freshly ground black pepper
1	teaspoon cinnamon
¼	teaspoon saffron, dissolved in 1 tablespoon hot water
1	teaspoon sugar
½	cup butter

Morgh-e Tu Por-e Torsh-o-Shirin

1. Clean and rinse chicken in cold water, then pat dry and rub it with ½ teaspoon salt.

2. Wash and chop chicken giblets; set aside.

3. Heat oil in a saucepan and brown onions and garlic. Add prunes, apple, apricots, raisins, 2 teaspoons salt, pepper, cinnamon, saffron and sugar. Mix well.

4. Stuff chicken with this mixture and pin or sew shut cavity.

5. Place the chicken in a buttered ovenproof dish or roasting pan and dot with butter. Cover with aluminum foil. Place in preheated 350°F oven and roast for 2 hours, basting occasionally with pan juices, or until meat separates easily from bone.

6. Serve chicken in ovenproof dish or arrange on a serving platter. Serve with *chelo* (page 95) or bread.

Stuffed Fish with Tamarind

1 large red snapper, about 5–6 pounds	3 cloves garlic, crushed
2 teaspoons salt	½ cup parsley
¼ pound tamarind	½ cup coriander
3 tablespoons butter or oil	2 tablespoons tomato paste
1 large onion, chopped	½ teaspoon turmeric
	¼ teaspoon pepper

Makes 4 servings
Preparation time: 15 min.
Cooking time: 1 hr.

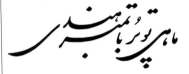

Mahi-ye Tu Por Ba Tamr-e Hendi

1. Soak tamarind in 1 cup of hot water for 1 hour. Over a bowl, pour tamarind through a strainer and discard the seeds.

2. Clean, scale and rinse fish in cold water. Pat dry with paper towel and rub inside and out with 1 teaspoon salt.

3. Set aside 2 tablespoons tamarind for garnish. Heat butter in a skillet and saute onion; add garlic, parsley, coriander, tomato paste, remaining tamarind, lemon juice, turmeric, 1 teaspoon salt and pepper. Cook for 5 minutes over low heat, stirring constantly.

4. Stuff fish with this mixture and arrange it in a baking dish. Pin or sew cavity shut. Dot fish with butter and 2 tablespoons of tamarind.

5. Place in preheated 350°F oven and bake for about 45 minutes to 1 hour, basting from time to time.

6. Arrange fish on serving platter and pour the pan sauce over it.

Stuffed Fish with Almonds

Makes 4 servings
Preparation time: 15 min.
Cooking time: 1 hr. 20 min.

1 large fish (sea bass, sea trout or rockfish), about 5–6 pounds
2 teaspoons salt
½ cup butter or oil
1 large onion, finely chopped
2 cloves garlic, crushed

½ cup slivered almonds
2 tablespoons chopped parsley
¼ teaspoon freshly ground black pepper
Juice of 2 lemons

Mahi-ye Tu Por Ba Badam

1. Clean, scale and rinse fish in cold water. Pat dry with a paper towel and rub inside and out with 1 teaspoon salt.

2. Heat ¼ cup butter in a large frying pan. Saute onion and garlic. Add almonds, parsley, 1 teaspoon salt and ¼ teaspoon pepper. Cook for 3 minutes.

3. Stuff fish with this mixture and sew or use a kitchen pin to shut the cavity. Arrange it in a buttered baking dish. Pour lemon juice and the rest of the butter over the fish.

4. Place in preheated 350°F oven and bake for 45 minutes to 1 hour (until the fish flakes easily with a fork), basting from time to time.

5. Arrange fish on serving platter and pour sauce from baking dish over fish.

Fish Stuffed with Fresh Herbs

Makes 6 servings
Preparation time: 30 min.
Cooking time: 40–60 min.,
depending on size of fish

1	large fish like sea bass, sea trout or rockfish, about 5–6 pounds
2	teaspoons salt
½	cup butter
½	cup parsley, chopped
2	tablespoons tarragon, chopped
4	scallions, chopped
1	tablespoon coriander, chopped
¼	cup chopped fresh mint or 2 tablespoons dried mint
2	cloves garlic, crushed
1	cup walnuts, finely chopped

¼	cup dried barberries, cleaned, washed and soaked in 1 cup water
¼	cup raisins
¼	cup lemon juice
¼	teaspoon freshly ground black pepper

GARNISH
2	tablespoons chopped radish greens
	Lemon slices

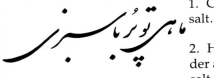

Mahi-ye Tu Por Ba Sabzi

1. Clean and scale fish; rinse and pat dry. Rub inside and out with 1 teaspoon salt.

2. Heat half the butter in skillet and saute parsley, tarragon, scallions, coriander and mint; add garlic, walnuts, barberries, raisins, lemon juice, 1 teaspoon salt and pepper. Mix well.

3. Fill the fish with stuffing; sew or use a kitchen pin to shut the cavity. Arrange the fish in a buttered baking dish. Dot fish with remaining butter. Place in preheated 350°F oven. Bake for 45 to 60 minutes (depending on size of fish), until the fish flakes easily with a fork, basting occasionally with the pan juices.

4. Arrange fish on a serving platter and garnish with radish greens and lemon slices.

5. Serve with *chelo* rice (page 95) or bread.

Note: If dried barberries are used, they must be soaked in a bowl of cold water for 10 minutes first. Lift out carefully, rinse and drain. Dried barberries are available in Middle Eastern food specialty shops (page 240).

Sauteed Lamb's Liver, Kidneys and Heart

1 lamb liver
2 lamb hearts
4 lamb kidneys
2 large onions, chopped
4 cloves garlic, chopped
5 tablespoons oil or butter
2 tablespoons tomato paste
1 tablespoon flour
2 tablespoons lemon juice

1½ teaspoons salt
½ teaspoon freshly ground black pepper
½ cup water
½ cup red wine (optional)
½ cup sliced cucumber pickles for garnish

Makes 4 servings
Preparation time: 15 min.
Cooking time: 15 min.

Khorak-e Del-o Jigar-o Gholveh

1. Slice liver and hearts lengthwise into strips 1 inch thick. Cut kidneys into 2-inch cubes. Wash and pat dry.

2. In a large skillet, brown meat, onions and garlic in the oil. Add tomato paste, 1 tablespoon flour, lemon juice, salt, pepper, ½ cup water and ½ cup red wine. Cover and simmer over medium heat for about 10 minutes.

3. Arrange on a serving platter and garnish with sliced cucumber pickles. Serve immediately.

Sauteed Brains

Makes 4 servings
Preparation time: 15 min.
Cooking time: 10 min.

4 lamb's brains
2 tablespoons vinegar
2 eggs
1 teaspoon salt
1 teaspoon freshly ground black pepper
3 tablespoons milk

1 onion, grated
¼ cup flour
½ cup dry bread crumbs
3 tablespoons oil
Juice of 2 lemons

Kotlet-e Maghz

1. Place brains in boiling water and 2 tablespoons vinegar for 1 minute. Remove membrane with a sharp knife and cut each brain in half.

2. Break eggs into a bowl. Add salt, pepper, milk and the grated onion. Beat well with a fork.

3. Sprinkle brains with flour. Dip into egg mixture and let excess drip off. Coat with bread crumbs.

4. Fry in a skillet in oil over low heat until golden brown.

5. Place on a serving dish, sprinkle with lemon juice and serve immediately with bread, fresh herbs and salad or steamed spinach and french fries.

Meat Patties

Makes 4 servings
Preparation time: 45 min.
Cooking time: 45 min.

1 large potato
1 pound ground lamb, veal or beef
1 medium onion, grated
1 egg
2 teaspoons salt
½ teaspoon freshly ground black pepper

½ teaspoon turmeric
¾ cup dry bread crumbs
¾ cup oil
4 ripe tomatoes, peeled and sliced (optional)
Parsley for garnish

Kotlet-e Gusht

1. Boil potato whole until cooked. Peel, mash and set aside.

2. In a bowl, combine meat, onion, egg, mashed potato, salt, pepper and turmeric. Knead for 10 minutes to form a smooth paste.

3. Using damp hands, shape mixture into lumps the size of an egg. Flatten and roll in bread crumbs. Brown on both sides in a skillet in ¼ cup hot oil over medium heat. Add more oil if necessary.

4. In another pan, saute the tomatoes in 2 tablespoons oil. Season with salt and pepper.

5. Arrange *kotlets* on a serving platter. Pour tomato sauce on top and garnish with parsley. Serve with French fries, bread, salad and fresh herbs and *torshi* (page 164).

Chick-pea Patties

Makes 4 servings
Preparation time: 10 min.
Cooking time: 20 min.

*Shami-e-Ard-e
Nokhodchi*

1 cup roasted chick-pea flour
⅔ cup warm water
½ teaspoon baking soda
1 pound ground lamb, beef or veal
2 large onions, finely grated
¼ teaspoon saffron, dissolved in 1 tablespoon hot water
¼ teaspoon ground cinnamon
¼ teaspoon ground nutmeg
1 teaspoon salt
¼ teaspoon freshly ground black pepper
½ cup oil or butter

GARNISH
Parsley sprigs
Lemon juice

SWEET AND SOUR SAUCE
1 onion, chopped
3 tablespoons oil
½ teaspoon turmeric
1 teaspoon dried mint
½ cup water
½ cup vinegar
½ cup sugar

1. Dissolve chick-pea flour in water and baking soda.

2. Add the meat, onions, saffron, cinnamon, nutmeg, salt and pepper and knead well with hands.

3. With damp hands, separate mixture into lumps the size of an orange. Flatten between palms into an oval shape and press a hole in the center with your finger. Fry on both sides in a skillet in hot oil over medium heat for about 5 minutes or until it is golden brown, adding more oil if necessary.

4. Arrange on a platter, garnish with parsley and lemon juice and serve very hot, warm or even cold with bread, *torshi* (page 164) and *sabzi khordan* (page 8).

5. *Shami* may also be served with a sweet and sour sauce. In a saucepan, fry 1 chopped onion in 3 tablespoons oil. Add turmeric, mint, water, vinegar and sugar and simmer over low heat for 15 minutes. Pour the sauce over *shami* before serving.

Note: Chick-pea flour is available in food specialty shops (page 240).

Tabriz-Style Meatballs

Makes 4 servings
Preparation time: 40 min.
Cooking time: 1 hr. 20 min.

6 eggs, 4 hard boiled and 2 slightly beaten
½ cup yellow split peas
3 large onions, 1 grated and 2 chopped
2 teaspoons salt
¼ teaspoon pepper
¼ teaspoon saffron dissolved in 1 tablespoon hot water
1 teaspoon *advieh* (allspice, page 160)
½ cup rice flour
1 pound ground meat
2 tablespoons dried marjoram or ¼ cup fresh chopped

2 cloves garlic, crushed
3 tablespoons oil or butter
2 cups beef broth
2 cups water or more, if necessary
1 teaspoon turmeric
1 tablespoon tomato paste
2 tablespoons lemon juice
¼ cup barberries, cleaned and washed
8 pieces pitted prunes
4 pieces walnut
4 pieces apricot

Koofteh Tabrizi

1. Hard boil 4 of the eggs. Shell and set aside.

2. Cook split peas for 20 minutes in 2 cups water and 1 teaspoon salt. Drain and set aside.

3. Beat 2 eggs in a large bowl. Add 1 grated onion, 1½ teaspoons salt, ¼ teaspoon pepper, saffron, allspice, rice flour, split peas, ground meat and chopped marjoram. Knead well for about 10 minutes until the mixture has reached the consistency of a smooth paste.

4. In a large pot, brown 2 chopped onions and garlic in oil. Add 2 cups beef broth, 2 cups water, turmeric, ½ teaspoon salt, the tomato paste and 2 tablespoons lemon juice. Bring to a boil.

5. Shape meat into 4 large balls the size of oranges. Stuff the center of each with 1 hard-boiled egg, 1 teaspoon barberries, 2 pieces of prune, 1 piece of walnut and 1 piece of apricot. Reshape the meat balls. Place in an ovenproof glass baking dish. Pour the boiling broth and onion mixture around the meatballs. Bake for 60 minutes or more in a preheated 350°F oven, turning the meatballs twice. Baste occasionally with pan juices to prevent them from drying out.

6. Check to see if meat is done. Taste sauce and adjust seasoning.

7. Serve in the same dish with bread and yogurt (page 212).

Variation: In a large pot, make your sauce and bring it to a boil. Gently place each meatball in the sauce and cook uncovered for 1½ to 2 hours, adding more water if necessary.

Note: If dried barberries are used, they must be soaked in a bowl of cold water for 10 minutes first. Lift out carefully, rinse and drain. Dried barberries and advieh are available in Middle Eastern food specialty shops (page 240).

Rice Meatballs

Makes 4 servings
Preparation time: 35 min.
Cooking time: 1 hr. 20 min.

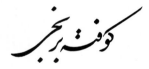

Koofteh Berenji

½ cup split peas
1 cup rice
¼ cup chopped parsley
¼ cup chopped mint
¼ cup chopped dill
¼ cup chopped marjoram
¼ cup chopped tarragon or 2 tablespoons dried
1 bunch scallions, chopped
3 eggs
1½ teaspoons salt
¼ teaspoon freshly ground black pepper
3 large onions (1 grated, 2 chopped)

1 pound ground meat
2 cloves garlic, crushed
½ cup oil
1 tablespoon tomato paste
2 cups water
2 cups beef broth
1 cup *gojeh sabs* (unripe plums) or ¼ cup lemon juice
1 teaspoon turmeric
¼ teaspoon saffron dissolved in 1 tablespoon hot water

1. Cook split peas and rice in a saucepan in 4 cups water with ½ teaspoon salt for 20 minutes. Drain and set aside.

2. Wash and chop parsley, mint, dill, marjoram, tarragon and scallions.

3. Break eggs into a bowl, add ½ teaspoon salt and the pepper and beat with a fork. Add 1 grated onion, ground meat, parsley, mint, dillweed, marjoram, tarragon, scallions, split peas and rice. Knead mixture thoroughly until it reaches the consistency of a smooth paste, about 10 minutes.

4. In a heavy pot, brown 2 chopped onions and garlic in the oil. Add tomato paste, 2 cups water, 2 cups beef broth, *gojeh sabs* or lemon juice, turmeric, 1 teaspoon salt and saffron. Bring to a boil.

5. Shape meat mixture into balls the size of an orange. Gently place each meatball into the boiling pot of broth. Cover and simmer gently for 1 hour over low heat, basting the meatballs occasionally with broth juices to prevent them from drying out. Uncover for the last 15 minutes of cooking.

6. Check to see if the meat is done and adjust seasoning. Place gently in a bowl and pour pan sauce on top. Serve hot with yogurt (page 212) and bread.

Note: *Gojeh sabs* are very sour green (unripe) plums, available fresh in season at food specialty stores (page 240).

Rice Meatballs
Koofteh Berenji
page 88

Jeweled Rice
Javaher Polo
page 112

Steamed Plain Rice
Chelo
page 95

Rice with Lentils and Dates
Adass Polo Ba Khorma
page 100

Ground Meat Brochettes

Makes 4 servings
Preparation time: 40 min.
Cooking time: 10 min.

Kabab-e Kubideh

Seasoned ground meat, molded on flat skewers and cooked on a charcoal fire, never fails to please. We mix lamb, which tends to be fatty, with lean beef or veal to get the proper texture. The right kind of skewers are sword-shaped. They can be found in Middle Eastern food shops (page 240) and sometimes with the gadgets in the housewares department of a hardware store.

1 **pound ground lamb**
1 **pound ground beef or veal**
1 **medium onion, grated**
1 **egg**
1 **tablespoon yogurt**
2 **teaspoons salt**
¼ **teaspoon freshly ground black pepper**

4 **tablespoons butter**
¼ **teaspoon saffron, dissolved in 1 tablespoon hot water**
2 **teaspoons powdered sumac or juice of 1 lime**

1. In a large bowl, combine meat, onion, egg, yogurt, salt and pepper. Knead with hands for 15 minutes to form a paste that will adhere well to the skewer. Cover and let age another 15 minutes at room temperature.

2. Using damp hands, divide mixture into 20 lumps about the size of an orange. Roll each into a sausage shape and mold firmly on skewer.

3. Melt butter in small saucepan and add dissolved saffron and a pinch of salt.

4. Start charcoal fire. When coals are evenly lit with white ash around each coal and the grill is very hot, arrange brochettes on grill 3 inches away from the coals; 2 seconds later, turn brochettes gently to prevent meat from falling off.

5. Grill brochettes 3 to 5 minutes on each side; avoid overcooking. The meat should be seared on the outside, juicy and tender on the inside. After cooking, remove from the barbecue and baste with melted butter and saffron sauce.

6. Slide the meat off the skewer using a piece of bread. Arrange on a serving platter, sprinkle with sumac or lime juice and cover brochettes with pieces of flat bread to keep them warm. Serve immediately with *chelo* (page 95) or bread, fresh herbs, scallions, salad, *mast-o khiar* (yogurt and cucumbers, page 12) and *torshi* (page 164).

Note: Sumac is sold ground like pepper in Middle Eastern food specialty stores (page 240).

Tongue with Tomato Sauce

Makes 4 servings
Preparation time: 20 min.
Cooking time: 4 hrs.

1 large beef or 2 calf's tongues
8 cups water
2 large onions, chopped
4 cloves garlic, crushed
2 bay leaves
4 cloves
¼ teaspoon pepper
3 tablespoons butter

3 tablespoons flour
2 tablespoons tomato paste
  Juice of 1 lemon
2 teaspoons salt
2 tablespoons chopped parsley
  for garnish

Khorak-e Zaban

1. Wash and rinse the tongue and place in a large pot. Add the water, onion, garlic, bay leaves, cloves and pepper and bring to a boil, skimming off the foam. Cover and simmer over low heat for 2½ hours for calf and 3½ hours for beef.

2. Remove the bay leaves and tongue from the broth and allow to cool. Remove the skin and excess fat off the tongue end and cut in thin slices.

3. In a saucepan, melt the butter, stir in the flour with a wire whisk and stir in the tomato paste. Place this mixture in the broth pot with the lemon juice; add salt and sliced tongue. Cover and simmer another ½ hour over low heat.

4. Arrange on a serving platter and garnish with parsley.

5. Serve hot with plenty of *torshi* (page 164), *sabzi khordan* (page 8) and warm bread.

R I C E

The Food of the Cloak

Mulla Nasrudin heard that there was a party being held in the nearby town, and that everyone was invited. He made his way there as quickly as he could. When the Master of Ceremonies saw him in his ragged cloak, he seated him in the most inconspicuous place, far from the great table where the most important people were being waited on hand and foot.

Mulla saw that it would be at least an hour before the waiters reached the place where he was sitting. So he got up and went home.

He dressed himself in a magnificent sable cloak and turban and returned to the feast. As soon as the heralds of the Emir, his host, saw this splendid sight they started to beat the drum of welcome and sound the trumpets in a manner consonant with a visitor of high rank.

The Chamberlain came out of the palace himself, and conducted the magnificent Nasrudin to a place almost next to the Emir. A dish of wonderful food was immediately placed before him. Without a pause, Nasrudin began to rub handfuls of it into his turban and cloak.

"Your eminence," said the prince, "I am curious as to your eating habits, which are new to me."

"Nothing special," said Mulla, "the cloak got me here, got me the food. Surely it deserves its share!"

R i c e

Rice has been grown in Persia for well over three thousand years. Long-grain rice is cultivated in northern Iran and plays a central role in the Persian diet and cuisine.

Chelo, the specially cooked rice that is served with *khoreshe* stews and *kababs*, is the jewel of Persian cuisine. Through a simple cooking process, the grains swell individually without sticking together. The result is light and fluffy rice.

After the rice is cooked, a layer of golden rice sticks to the bottom of the saucepan. This tasty, crisp crust is called *tah digue*. It should be a golden color, never scorched or dark brown. The reputation of Iranian cooks rests on the quality of their *tah digue* or golden crust.

Basmati rice, from India, is very close to Persian rice. It is named after the basmati flower, a lovely perfumed tropical bloom found in India. When basmati rice is cooked, it fills the air with a delightful aroma similar to that of the flower. Other kinds of long-grain rice may also be used for Persian rice dishes, but never the so-called converted rice (Uncle Ben's brand, for example).

Saffron imparts the golden color and special flavor that is so prized by connoisseurs. The saffron is ground into a very fine powder and dissolved in a little hot water before being added to the rice.

A deep non-stick saucepan must be used for the rice grains to swell properly and a good *tah digue* to form without sticking. An electric rice cooker can also produce excellent *chelo*.

A Note on Storing Rice: The best available rice for making Persian-style *polo* (cooked rice) is basmati rice from India. There are several U.S. distributors for basmati rice, including A&A Food Products Division of Richter Brothers, Inc., Carlstadt, N.J. 07072, and House of Spices, 76-17 Broadway, Jackson Heights, N.Y. 11373. I find it convenient to buy the large 55-pound sack and store the rice in a big popcorn tin with a cover. The rice should be mixed first with 1 pound of salt to repel bugs and keep mold from forming. Basmati rice is also sold in 11-pound sacks and 5-pound plastic bags. The rice should always be well cleaned and washed immediately before cooking.

A Note on Washing Rice: Basmati rice, which is similar to Persian rice, contains many small solid particles. This grit must be removed by picking over the rice carefully by hand. Then the rice is washed thoroughly in cold water. Place the rice in a large pot and cover with cold water. Agitate briskly with your hand, then pour off the water. Repeat 5 times until the rice is completely clean. When washed rice is cooked, it gives off a delightful perfume that unwashed rice can never have.

A Note on Rice Cooking Times: Throughout this book I have used cooking times for Basmati rice, which I recommend. However, if you use American Long-Grain rice, then in step 2 of the recipes increase the boiling period for the rice from 6 to 10 minutes.

A Note On Rice Cookers: Rice cookers are a wonderful invention for cooking rice Persian style because the non-stick coated mold allows for a golden crust (*tah-dig*) and as the temperature does not vary it allows for consistently good rice. However, each type of rice cooker seems to have its own temperature setting and therefore the timing must be experimented with to get the best results.

Step by step instructions are given for Steamed Plain Rice (page 96) and Rice with Lentils (page 102) using the National Delux electric rice cooker. Other rice recipes can similarly be carried out. Electric rice cookers are available at specialty food stores (page 240).

Steamed Plain Rice

Makes 6 servings
Preparation time: 5 min. plus 2
hrs. soaking time (optional)
Cooking time: 1 hr. 10 min.

3 cups long-grain rice (*basmati*)
8 cups water
2 tablespoons salt
¾ cup melted butter
½ teaspoon ground saffron,
　dissolved in 2 tablespoons hot
　water
2 tablespoons yogurt (optional)

Chelo

1. Clean and wash 3 cups of rice 5 times in cold water. It is then desirable but not essential to soak the rice in 8 cups of water with 2 tablespoons of salt for at least 2 hours.

2. Bring 8 cups water and 2 tablespoons salt to a boil in a large non-stick pot. Pour the washed and drained rice into the pot. Boil briskly for 6 minutes, stirring gently twice to loosen any grains that may have stuck to the bottom. Drain rice in a colander and rinse in lukewarm water.

3. In the same pot, heat half the butter, 2 tablespoons hot water, a drop of dissolved saffron and yogurt.

4. Take one spatula full of drained rice at a time and gently place it in this pot, mounding it in the shape of a pyramid.

5. Dissolve the remaining butter in 2 tablespoons hot water and pour over the rice pyramid. Place a clean dishtowel or paper towel over the pot and cover firmly with lid to prevent steam from escaping. Cook 10 minutes over medium heat and 50 minutes over low heat. Remove from heat.

6. Allow to cool for 5 minutes on a damp surface without opening. Put 2 tablespoons of rice in a dish, mix with remaining saffron and set aside for use as a garnish.

7. Gently taking one skimmer or spatula full of rice at a time, place it in an oval serving platter without disturbing the crust. Mound the rice in the shape of a cone. Sprinkle the saffron-flavored rice over the top and serve.

8. Detach the bottom layer using a wooden spatula. Unmold onto a small platter and serve on the side.

Steamed Plain Rice: Electric Rice Cooker Method

3 cups long-grain rice
3 cups water
1 tablespoon salt
¼ cup oil
½ cup butter
¼ teaspoon ground saffron dissolved in 1 tablespoon hot water

Makes 6 servings
Preparation time: 10 min. plus 2 hrs. soaking time (optional)
Cooking time: 1 hr. 30 min.

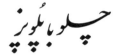

Chelo Ba Polo Paz

1. Clean and wash 3 cups of rice 5 times in cold water.

2. Combine all the ingredients except the saffron in the rice cooker and start it.

3. After 90 minutes, pour dissolved saffron on top of rice. Unplug the rice cooker.

4. Allow to cool for 10 minutes without opening.

5. Remove lid and place a round serving dish over the pot. Hold the dish and the pot tightly and turn over to unmold rice. The rice will be like a cake. Cut it in wedges and serve.

Note: These cooking times are for the National Delux Rice Cooker. The cooking time for rice varies between the different brands of rice cookers (see page 94).

Smothered Rice

3 **cups long-grain rice**
1 **tablespoon salt**
6 **cups water**
½ **cup butter**
2 **tablespoons oil**

Makes 6 servings
Preparation time: 5 min. plus 2
hrs. soaking time (optional)
Cooking time: 1 hr.

Kateh

1. Clean and wash 3 cups of rice 5 times in cold water.

2. Place rice, 1 tablespoon salt and 6 cups of water in a deep non-stick pot. Bring to a boil, then reduce heat and simmer for 20 minutes over medium heat (do not cover the rice), gently stirring the rice twice while it boils.

3. When rice has absorbed all water, put butter and oil on top.

4. Place a clean dishtowel or paper towel over pot and cover firmly with lid to prevent steam from escaping. Cook 40 minutes over low heat. Remove from heat and allow to cool for 5 minutes on a damp surface without opening.

5. Gently taking one skimmer or spatula full of rice at a time, place it in an oval serving platter without disturbing crust. Mound rice in shape of a cone.

6. Detach bottom layer using a wooden spatula. Unmold onto a small platter and serve on side.

Oven-Baked Rice

Makes 6 servings
Preparation time: 1 hr. 40 min.
plus 2 hrs. soaking time (optional)
Cooking time: 1 hr. 30 min.

3 cups long-grain rice
1 chicken, about 2 pounds
1 onion, finely chopped
1 eggplant
3 tablespoons oil
1 cup barberries (*zereshke*)
¾ cup butter
2 tablespoons sugar

½ teaspoon ground saffron, dissolved in 2 tablespoons hot water
½ cup yogurt
2 egg yolks

Shirazy Polo

1. Clean and wash 3 cups of rice 5 times in cold water. It is then desirable but not essential to soak the rice in 8 cups of water with 2 tablespoons of salt for at least 2 hours.

2. Place the chicken and onion in a saucepan. Do not add water. Cover and simmer 45 minutes over low heat. Bone the chicken and cut it into pieces. Set aside, reserving juice.

3. Peel and slice the eggplant crosswise. Sprinkle with salt, set aside for 20 minutes, then rinse and pat dry. Brown in hot oil in a skillet. Set aside a few slices for garnish.

4. Clean barberries by removing their stems and washing thoroughly in cold water. Soak in cold water for 10 minutes, then drain carefully, leaving the sand behind. Saute in a skillet in 2 tablespoons butter. Remove from heat and add the sugar and half the dissolved saffron. Set aside some of the berries for garnish.

5. Bring 8 cups water and 2 tablespoons salt to a boil in a large non-stick pot. Pour the washed and drained rice into the pot. Boil briskly for 6 minutes, stirring gently twice to loosen any grains that may have stuck to the bottom. Drain rice in a colander and rinse in lukewarm water.

6. Melt remaining butter in a deep ovenproof dish that has a lid.

7. Take 3 spatulas full of rice and combine with yogurt, egg yolk and remaining saffron. Place the rice mixture in the ovenproof dish. Arrange chicken pieces on top. Pour the barberry mixture over the chicken. Arrange a few slices of eggplant on top. Cover with remaining rice. Pour the chicken juice over the rice and pack down into dish, using a spoon.

8. Place lid on ovenproof dish to prevent steam from escaping. Bake in a preheated 350°F oven for 1 to 1½ hours.

9. Remove from oven and allow to cool for 10 minutes on a damp surface. Loosen the rice around the edges of the dish with the point of a knife. Place a large serving platter on top of the dish. Hold the dish and platter firmly together and turn over to unmold the rice. Garnish with the reserved eggplant slices and spoon barberries on top of the rice.

10. Serve hot.

Rice with Lentils

Makes 6 servings
Preparation time: 1 hr. 15 min.
plus 2 hrs. soaking time (optional)
Cooking time: 1 hr.

3	cups long-grain rice	
2	onions, finely chopped	
2	tablespoons oil	
1½	pounds leg, shoulder or shank of lamb	
1	teaspoon salt	
¼	teaspoon freshly ground black pepper	
½	teaspoon turmeric	

1 teaspoon cinnamon
½ teaspoon ground saffron, dissolved in 2 tablespoons hot water
1 cup lentils
1 cup melted butter
2 tablespoons yogurt (optional)
½ cup raisins
2 cups pitted dates

Adass Polo

1. Clean and wash 3 cups of rice 5 times in cold water. It is then desirable but not essential to soak the rice in 8 cups of water with 2 tablespoons of salt for at least 2 hours.

2. In a saucepan, saute the finely chopped onions in 2 tablespoons oil; add the meat. Season with 1 teaspoon salt, ¼ teaspoon pepper, turmeric and cinnamon. Pour in 1 cup water. Cover and simmer 1 hour over low heat. Add a third of the saffron.

3. Cook lentils about 10 minutes in 3 cups water and ½ teaspoon salt. Drain.

4. Bring 8 cups water and 2 tablespoons salt to a boil in a large non-stick pot. Pour the washed and drained rice into the pot. Boil briskly for 6 minutes, stirring gently twice to loosen any grains that may have stuck to the bottom. Drain rice in a colander and rinse in lukewarm water.

5. In the same saucepan, heat half the butter, a third of the saffron and yogurt.

6. Sprinkle 2 spatulas full of rice in the pot. Add a few pieces of meat, 1 spatula full of lentils, the raisins and dates. Repeat, arranging the rice in the shape of a pyramid.

7. Pour the remaining melted butter, 2 tablespoons of the meat juices and the remaining saffron over this pyramid.

8. Place a clean dishtowel or paper towel over the pot and cover firmly with lid to prevent steam from escaping. Cook 10 minutes over medium heat and 50 minutes over low heat. Remove from heat and allow to cool for 5 minutes on a damp surface without opening.

9. Open the pot, take 2 tablespoons of the saffron-flavored rice and set aside for garnishing.

10. Gently taking one skimmer or spatula full of rice at a time, place it in an oval serving platter without disturbing the crust. Mound the rice in the shape of a cone. Decorate with saffron-flavored rice.

11. Detach the bottom layer crust using a wooden spatula. Unmold onto a small platter and serve on the side.

Variation

Rice with Noodles

Reshteh Polo

Reshteh Polo can be made by following the steps for Adass Polo except that in step 3, ½ lb. of pre-prepared browned Persian noodles (*reshteh*) cut in 1-inch lengths can replace the lentils. All cooking times, proportions and spices stay the same.

Rice with Lentils: Electric Rice Cooker Method

3 cups long-grain rice
1 teaspoon salt
½ cup oil
2 finely chopped onions
2 pounds leg, shoulder or shank of lamb
¼ teaspoon freshly ground black pepper

1 teaspoon cinnamon
½ teaspoon turmeric
½ teaspoon saffron dissolved in 2 tablespoons hot water
1 cup lentils
½ cup butter
½ cup black raisins
2 cups pitted dates

Makes 6 servings
Preparation time: 1 hr. 15 min.
plus 2 hrs. soaking time (optional)
Cooking time: 1 hr.

عدس پلو با پلوپز

Adass Polo Ba Polo Paz

1. Clean and wash 3 cups of rice 5 times in cold water. Combine with 4 cups water and 1 level tablespoon salt in the non-stick rice cooker mold.

2. In a saucepan, saute onions in 3 tablespoons oil, then add the meat. Season with 1 teaspoon salt, pepper, cinnamon and turmeric. Add 1½ cups water, bring to a boil, reduce heat and cover and simmer for 45 minutes over low heat. Add a drop of saffron.

3. Start the electric rice cooker. Cover and let cook for about 20 minutes or until the water is almost absorbed, stirring gently once with a wooden spatula to loosen any grains that may have stuck to the bottom. Drain rice in a colander and rinse in lukewarm water.

4. Clean and wash lentils and boil in 4 cups water and ½ teaspoon salt for 10 minutes. Drain and set aside.

5. Place half the butter and remaining oil and half the dissolved saffron in the rice cooker mold. Place 2 spatulas full of rice on top. Add a few pieces of meat, 1 large spoonful of lentils, the raisins and dates.

6. Repeat these steps, arranging the rice in the shape of a pyramid. Pour the remaining melted butter, 2 tablespoons of the meat juices and dissolved saffron over the pyramid.

7. Cover and cook for 60 minutes, then unplug cooker and let stand for 10 minutes without opening.

8. Remove lid, place large serving dish on top. Grasp firmly and turn pot upside down to unmold rice on dish. Cut in wedges to serve.

Note: The cooking times are for the National Delux Rice Cooker. The cooking time for rice varies between the different brands of rice cookers (see page 94).

Rice with Dried Yellow Fava Beans

Makes 6 servings
Preparation time: 45 min. plus 2 hrs. soaking time (optional)
Cooking time: 1 hr.

3 cups long-grain rice
2 onions, chopped
¼ cup oil
1 tablespoon turmeric
1 cup dried yellow fava beans
1 teaspoon salt
¼ teaspoon freshly ground black pepper
½ cup butter, cut in pieces

GARNISH
½ cup raisins
½ cup pitted dates
2 eggs, fried sunny side up (optional)

Dampokhtak

1. Clean and wash 3 cups of rice 5 times in cold water.

2. In a deep non-stick pot, brown the chopped onions in 3 tablespoons oil. Add turmeric, beans, 2 cups water, 1 teaspoon salt and ¼ teaspoon pepper. Cover and simmer over medium heat for 45 minutes.

3. Add the rice, 4 cups water and 1 tablespoon salt to the pot and simmer 20 minutes over medium heat. As soon as the water has evaporated, pour butter and the rest of the oil on top of the rice.

4. Place a clean dishtowel or paper towel over the pot and cover firmly with lid to prevent steam from escaping. Cook 40 minutes over low heat. Remove from heat and allow to cool for 5 minutes on a damp surface without opening.

5. Gently taking one skimmer or spatula full of rice at a time, place it in an oval serving platter without disturbing the crust. Mound the rice in the shape of a cone. Garnish with raisins, dates and sunny-side-up fried eggs.

6. Detach the bottom layer using a wooden spatula. Unmold onto a small platter and serve on the side.

7. Serve immediately with *torshi* (Persian pickles, page 164) and *sabzi-khordan* (fresh vegetables and herbs, page 8).

Rice with Sour Cherries

*Makes 6 servings
Preparation time: 1 hr. 30 min.
plus 2 hrs. soaking time (optional)
Cooking time: 1 hr.*

Albalou Polo

3 cups long-grain rice
10 cups fresh or frozen sour cherries, cleaned, washed and pitted or 4 cans, 1 pound each, red tart pitted cherries packed in water
4 cups sugar
1 chicken, about 3 pounds cut up
2 large onions, 1 finely chopped, 1 grated
½ teaspoon ground saffron, dissolved in 2 tablespoons hot water
½ pound ground meat (lamb, veal or beef)

1¼ teaspoons salt
¼ teaspoon freshly ground black pepper
2 tablespoons oil
½ cup butter
2 tablespoons yogurt

GARNISH
1 tablespoon slivered almonds
1 tablespoon slivered pistachios
2 tablespoons hot melted butter
2 tablespoons cherry syrup

1. Clean and wash 3 cups of rice 5 times in cold water. It is then desirable but not essential to soak the rice in 8 cups of water with 2 tablespoons of salt for at least 2 hours.

2. Place washed and pitted cherries and sugar in a saucepan. Cook for 35 minutes over medium heat. Set aside to cool. Separate the cherries, and reserve the syrup.

3. In a saucepan, cook the chicken with a finely chopped onion and 1 teaspoon salt. Do not add water; the chicken will produce its own juice. Cover and simmer 45 minutes over low heat. Bone the chicken and cut it into pieces. Add a drop of dissolved saffron. Set aside.

4. In a bowl, combine the ground meat and one peeled, grated onion. Add ¼ teaspoon salt and ¼ teaspoon pepper. Knead well and form into tiny balls the size of a hazelnut. Brown in a skillet in oil. Set aside.

5. Bring 8 cups water and 2 tablespoons salt to a boil in a large non-stick pot. Pour the washed and drained rice into the pot. Boil briskly for 6 minutes, stirring gently twice to loosen any grains that may have stuck to the bottom. Drain rice in a colander and rinse in lukewarm water.

6. In the same pot, heat half the butter, a drop of dissolved saffron and yogurt.

7. Place 2 spatulas full of rice in the pot, then 1 spatula of cherries. Place the pieces of chicken and meatballs on top. (Set aside 1 large spoonful of cherries, a few pieces of chicken and several meatballs for garnish.)

8. Repeat these steps, arranging the rice in the shape of a pyramid. Pour the remaining butter and saffron and 2 tablespoons of chicken juice over this pyramid.

9. Place a clean dishtowel or paper towel over the pot and cover firmly with lid to prevent steam from escaping. Cook 10 minutes over medium heat and 50 minutes over low heat. Remove from heat and allow to cool for 5 minutes on a damp surface without opening.

10. Remove lid and take 2 tablespoons of saffron-flavored rice and set aside with the cherries, chicken pieces and meatballs that were reserved for garnishing.

11. Gently taking one skimmer or spatula full of rice at a time, place it in an oval serving platter without disturbing the crust. Mound the rice in the shape of a cone. Garnish with saffron-flavored rice, chicken pieces, meatballs, almonds and pistachio nuts. Pour ½ cup hot cherry syrup over rice.

12. Detach the bottom layer using a wooden spatula. Unmold onto a small platter and serve on the side.

Variation: Two 1-lb. jars of good sour-cherry preserves, with whole cherries, may be used instead of step 2. Specialty food stores often carry high-quality imported brands. Frozen sour cherries may also be used, and are available at Middle Eastern food specialty shops (page 240).

Rice and Baby Lima Beans

Makes 6 servings
Preparation time: 1 hr. plus 2 hrs.
soaking time (optional)
Cooking time: 1 hr.

3 cups long-grain rice
1 pound fresh or frozen baby lima beans, shelled
2 onions, finely chopped
2 pounds leg or shank of lamb, beef or veal
¾ cup butter or oil

½ teaspoon salt
½ teaspoon ground saffron, dissolved in 2 tablespoons hot water
2 tablespoons yogurt
2 cups chopped fresh dill

Baghla Polo

1. Clean and wash 3 cups of rice 5 times in cold water. It is then desirable but not essential to soak the rice in 8 cups of water with 2 tablespoons of salt for at least 2 hours.

2. Shell lima beans and remove outer layer of skin. (If frozen beans are used, you do not have to remove skin.)

3. In a saucepan, saute onion with the pieces of meat in 3 tablespoons butter. Add 1 cup water, ½ teaspoon salt and a little dissolved saffron. Cover and simmer 45 minutes over low heat.

4. Bring 8 cups water and 2 tablespoons salt to a boil in a large non-stick pot. Pour the washed and drained rice into the pot. Boil briskly for 6 minutes, stirring gently twice to loosen any grains that may have stuck to the bottom. Drain rice in a colander and rinse in lukewarm water.

5. In the same pot, heat half the butter, a drop of dissolved saffron and yogurt.

6. Place 2 spatulas full of rice in the pot, then spread 1 spoonful of chopped dill, 1 spoonful of beans and the cooked meat on top. Repeat, arranging the rice in the shape of a pyramid. Pour the remaining butter, saffron and 2 tablespoons of meat juices over this pyramid.

7. Place a clean dishtowel or paper towel over the pot and cover firmly with lid to prevent steam from escaping. Cook 10 minutes over medium heat and 50 minutes over low heat. Remove from heat and allow to cool for 5 minutes on a damp surface without opening.

8. Remove lid and take 2 tablespoons of saffron-flavored rice and set aside for use as a garnish.

9. Gently taking a skimmer or spatula full of rice at a time, place it in an oval serving platter without disturbing the crust. Mound the rice in the shape of a cone. Garnish with the mixture of rice and saffron.

10. Detach the bottom layer using a wooden spatula. Unmold onto a small platter and serve on the side.

Sweet Rice

Makes 6 servings
Preparation time: 1 hr. 10 min.
plus 2 hrs. soaking time (optional)
Cooking time: 1 hr.

3 cups long-grain rice
2 pounds ground lamb, veal or beef or 1 fryer chicken, about 3 pounds, cut up
1 onion, chopped
1 teaspoon salt
¼ teaspoon freshly ground black pepper
½ cup butter
2 cups slivered orange peel
2 cups sugar

6 carrots, cut into thin strips
2 tablespoons chopped pistachios
½ cup slivered almonds
½ teaspoon ground saffron, dissolved in 2 tablespoons hot water
2 tablespoons yogurt
1 teaspoon *advieh* (allspice, page 160)

Shirin Polo

1. Clean and wash 3 cups of rice 5 times in cold water. It is then desirable but not essential to soak the rice in 8 cups of water with 2 tablespoons of salt for at least 2 hours.

2. In a bowl, combine the ground meat and onion. Season to taste with 1 teaspoon salt and ¼ teaspoon pepper. Knead well and form the mixture into meatballs the size of a chestnut. Brown in a skillet in 2 tablespoons butter. Set aside. (If you are using chicken, place it with the chopped onion, cover and simmer for 45 minutes over low heat. It will produce its own juice.)

3. Boil the slivered orange peel in 3 cups of water for 5 minutes and drain. In a saucepan, place the orange peel, sugar, carrots and 3 cups water and let boil for 15 minutes. Drain, add chopped pistachios and slivered almonds and set aside.

4. Bring 8 cups water and 2 tablespoons salt to a boil in a large non-stick pot. Pour the washed and drained rice into the pot. Boil briskly for 6 minutes, stirring gently twice to loosen any grains that may have stuck to the bottom. Drain rice in a colander and rinse in lukewarm water.

5. In the same pot, heat half the butter, a drop of dissolved saffron and yogurt.

6. Place 2 spatulas full of rice in the pot, then add the meatballs or chicken and the carrot mixture. Set aside 4 tablespoons of this mixture for use as a garnish. Repeat these steps, arranging the rice in the shape of a pyramid and sprinkling 1 teaspoon *advieh* over it. Pour the remaining butter and saffron over this pyramid. Add meat or chicken juices.

7. Place a clean dishtowel or paper towel over the pot and cover firmly with lid to prevent steam from escaping. Cook 10 minutes over medium heat and 50 minutes over low heat. Remove from heat and allow to cool for 5 minutes on a damp surface without opening.

8. Remove lid and take 2 tablespoons of saffron-flavored rice and set aside for use as a garnish.

9. Gently taking one skimmer or spatula full of rice at a time, place it in an oval serving platter without disturbing the crust. Mound the rice in the shape of a cone. Garnish with saffroned flavor rice and the mixture of orange peel, pistachios, almonds and carrots.

10. Detach the bottom layer using a wooden spatula. Unmold onto a small platter and serve on the side.

Note: *Advieh* is available at food specialty shops (page 240).

Rice with Green Peas

Makes 6 servings
Preparation time: 1 hr. plus 2 hrs.
soaking time (optional)
Cooking time: 1 hr.

Nokhod Polo

3 cups long-grain rice (*basmati*)
1 fryer chicken, about 3 pounds
   or 2 pounds shank or
   shoulder of lamb or beef chuck
1 onion, chopped
½ teaspoon salt
¼ teaspoon freshly ground black
   pepper
¼ teaspoon ground saffron,
   dissolved in 1 tablespoon hot
   water

2 cups fresh or frozen peas
2 cups fresh dill, chopped, or 6
   tablespoons dried
½ cup butter
2 tablespoons yogurt

1. Clean and wash 3 cups of rice 5 times in cold water. It is then desirable but not essential to soak the rice in 8 cups of water with 2 tablespoons of salt for at least 2 hours.

2. Put the chicken or meat in a pot with the onion and add ½ teaspoon salt and ¼ teaspoon pepper. Cover and simmer 45 minutes over low heat. Bone the chicken and cut into pieces. Add a third of the saffron. Set aside.

3. Cook peas in ½ cup water for 10 minutes. Drain and mix with the chopped dill.

4. Bring 8 cups water and 2 tablespoons salt to a boil in a large non-stick pot. Pour the washed and drained rice into the pot. Boil briskly for 6 minutes, stirring gently twice to loosen any grains that may have stuck to the bottom. Drain rice in a colander and rinse in lukewarm water.

5. In the same pot, heat half the butter, a drop of dissolved saffron and yogurt.

6. Place 2 spatulas full of rice in the pot, then add 1 spoonful of chicken or meat pieces, 1 spoonful of peas and the dill. Repeat these steps, arranging the rice in the shape of a pyramid. Pour the remaining butter, saffron and the chicken or meat juices over this pyramid.

7. Place a clean dishtowel or paper towel over the pot and cover firmly with lid to prevent steam from escaping. Cook 10 minutes over medium heat and 50 minutes over low heat.

8. Before serving, remove rice pot from heat and allow to cool for 5 minutes on a damp surface without opening.

9. Remove lid, take 2 tablespoons of saffron-flavored rice and set aside for garnishing.

10. Gently taking one skimmer or spatula full of rice at a time, place it in an oval serving platter without disturbing the crust. Mound the rice in the shape of a cone. Garnish with the saffron-flavored rice.

11. Detach the bottom layer using a wooden spatula. Unmold onto a small platter and serve on the side.

12. Serve with *torshi* (Persian pickles, page 164) and *sabzi-khordan* (fresh vegetables and herbs, page 8).

Jeweled Rice

Makes 6 servings
Preparation time: 1 hr. 10 min.
plus 2 hrs. soaking time (optional)
Cooking time: 1 hr.

Javaher Polo

3 cups long-grain rice
1 fryer chicken, about 3 pounds, cut up
2 onions, chopped
½ teaspoon salt
1 cup very finely slivered orange peel
2 carrots, peeled and cut into thin slivers
1 cup sugar
½ cup raisins
1 cup dried barberries, cleaned, washed and soaked for 10 minutes

½ cup butter
½ teaspoon ground saffron, dissolved in 2 tablespoons hot water
2 tablespoons yogurt (optional)
1 teaspoon *advieh* (allspice, page 160)
2 tablespoons slivered almonds
2 tablespoons pistachio nuts

1. Clean and wash 3 cups of rice 5 times in cold water. It is then desirable but not essential to soak the rice in 8 cups of water with 2 tablespoons of salt for at least 2 hours.

2. Put the chicken and 1 chopped onion in a saucepan. Add ½ teaspoon salt, cover and simmer for 45 minutes over low heat (do not add water). Bone chicken and cut into pieces.

3. Cover the slivered orange peel with water, bring to a boil and drain to remove bitter taste. Place the orange peel, carrot strips, 1 cup sugar and 1 cup water in a saucepan and boil for 10 minutes. Drain and set aside.

4. Saute one chopped onion, raisins and drained barberries in 4 tablespoons butter for 2 minutes in a skillet. Add orange peel and carrots and set aside.

5. Bring 8 cups water and 2 tablespoons salt to a boil in a large non-stick pot. Pour the washed and drained rice into the pot. Boil briskly for 6 minutes, stirring gently twice to loosen any grains that may have stuck to the bottom. Drain rice in a colander and rinse in lukewarm water.

6. In the same saucepan, heat half the remaining butter, a drop of dissolved saffron and yogurt.

7. Place 2 spatulas full of rice in the pot, then add a few pieces of chicken. Repeat these steps, arranging the rice in the shape of a pyramid. Sprinkle 1 teaspoon *advieh* over the rice. Pour the rest of the butter and saffron and 2 tablespoons of the chicken juices over this pyramid.

8. Place a clean dishtowel or paper towel over the pot and cover firmly with lid to prevent steam from escaping. Cook 10 minutes over medium heat and 50 minutes over low heat. Remove from heat and allow to cool for 5 minutes on a damp surface without opening.

9. Remove lid and take 2 tablespoons of saffron-flavored rice and set aside for use as a garnish.

10. Then, gently taking one spatula full of rice at a time, place it in an oval serving platter in alternating layers with the chicken and barberry mixture. Mound the rice in the shape of a cone. Finally, decorate the top of the mound with the saffron-flavored rice, some of the barberry mixture, and almonds and pistachios.

11. Detach the bottom layer using a wooden spatula. Unmold onto a small platter and serve on the side.

Note: *Advieh* is available at food specialty stores (page 240).

Rice with Yellow Split Peas

Makes 6 servings
Preparation time: 1 hr. 10 min.
plus 2 hrs. soaking time (optional)
Cooking time: 1 hr.

Gheimeh Polo

3 cups long-grain rice
2 large onions, chopped
1½ pounds stewing meat, lamb, veal or beef, cut in ½-inch cubes
3 tablespoons oil
½ teaspoon turmeric
1 teaspoon salt
¼ teaspoon freshly ground black pepper
½ cup yellow split peas

2 tablespoons tomato paste
1 tablespoon powdered *limou-omani* (dried Persian limes)
½ cup butter
½ teaspoon ground saffron, dissolved in 2 tablespoons hot water
2 tablespoons yogurt
1 teaspoon *advieh* (allspice, page 160)

1. Clean and wash 3 cups of rice 5 times in cold water. It is then desirable but not essential to soak the rice in 8 cups of water with 2 tablespoons of salt for at least 2 hours.

2. In a saucepan, brown the onions and meat in 3 tablespoons oil. Add turmeric, 1 teaspoon salt, ¼ teaspoon pepper and 2 cups water. Bring to a boil, cover and simmer over medium heat for 30 minutes. Add split peas, tomato paste and powdered *limou-omani*. Cover and simmer for 30 minutes longer over low heat.

3. Bring 8 cups water and 2 tablespoons salt to a boil in a large non-stick pot. Pour the washed and drained rice into the pot. Boil briskly for 6 minutes, stirring gently twice to loosen any grains that may have stuck to the bottom. Drain rice in a colander and rinse in lukewarm water.

4. In the same pot, heat half the butter, a drop of dissolved saffron and yogurt.

5. Place 2 spatulas full of rice in the pot, then add some meat and split pea mixture. Repeat these steps, arranging the rice in the shape of a pyramid. Pour the remaining butter and saffron over this pyramid. Sprinkle with *advieh*.

6. Place a clean dishtowel or paper towel over the pot and cover firmly with lid to prevent steam from escaping. Cook 10 minutes over medium heat and 50 minutes over low heat. Remove from heat and allow to cool for 5 minutes on a damp surface without opening.

7. Remove lid and take 2 tablespoons of saffron-flavored rice and set aside for use as a garnish.

8. Then, gently taking one skimmer or spatula full of rice at a time, place it in an oval serving platter without disturbing the crust. Mound the rice in the shape of a cone and garnish with the saffron-flavored rice.

9. Detach the bottom layer using a wooden spatula. Unmold onto a small platter and serve on the side.

Note: *Advieh* is available at specialty food shops (page 240).

Rice with Green Cabbage

Makes 6 servings
Preparation time: 1 hr. plus 2 hrs.
soaking time (optional)
Cooking time: 1 hr.

Kalame Polo

3 cups long-grain rice
1 pound ground lamb, veal or beef
1 onion, grated
½ teaspoon salt
¼ teaspoon freshly ground black pepper
3 tablespoons oil
1 large head green cabbage, shredded
1 tablespoon ground cumin (optional)

1 tablespoon tomato paste or 2 fresh tomatoes, peeled and chopped
½ teaspoon ground saffron, dissolved in 2 tablespoons hot water
½ cup butter
2 tablespoons yogurt
1 teaspoon *advieh* (allspice, page 160)

1. Clean and wash 3 cups of rice 5 times in cold water. It is then desirable but not essential to soak the rice in 8 cups of water with 2 tablespoons of salt for at least 2 hours.

2. In a bowl, combine the ground meat and grated onion. Season with ½ teaspoon salt and ¼ teaspoon pepper. Knead well and form the mixture into meatballs the size of a chestnut.

3. Brown the meatballs in a saucepan in 3 tablespoons oil. Add the cabbage, cumin, tomato paste and ½ cup water. Cook for 10 minutes over medium heat.

4. Bring 8 cups water and 2 tablespoons salt to a boil in a large non-stick pot. Pour the washed and drained rice into the pot. Boil briskly for 6 minutes, stirring gently twice to loosen any grains that may have stuck to the bottom. Drain rice in a colander and rinse in lukewarm water.

5. In the same pot, heat half the butter, a drop of dissolved saffron and yogurt.

6. Place 2 spatulas full of rice in the pot, then add the cabbage and meatball mixture. Repeat these steps, arranging the rice in the shape of a pyramid. Pour the remaining butter and saffron over this pyramid and sprinkle *advieh* over it.

7. Place a clean dishtowel or paper towel over the pot and cover firmly with lid to prevent steam from escaping. Cook 10 minutes over medium heat and 50 minutes over low heat. Remove from heat and allow to cool for 5 minutes on a damp surface without opening.

8. Set aside 2 tablespoons of saffron-flavored rice for use as a garnish. Then, gently taking one skimmer or spatula full of rice at a time, place it in an oval serving platter without disturbing the crust. Mound the rice in the shape of a cone. Garnish with the saffroned rice.

9. Detach the bottom layer using a wooden spatula. Unmold onto a small platter and serve on the side.

Note: *Advieh* is available at food specialty stores (page 240).

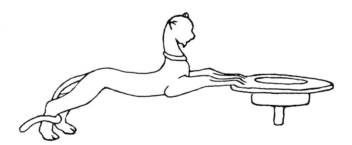

Rice with Green Beans

Makes 6 servings
Preparation time: 1 hr. plus 2 hrs.
soaking time (optional)
Cooking time: 1 hr.

3 cups long-grain rice
1 onion, finely chopped
1½ pounds stewing meat,
   cut in ½-inch cubes
5 tablespoons oil
2 tomatoes, peeled and sliced
1 tablespoon tomato paste
1½ pounds green beans, cleaned
   and cut in ½-inch pieces

1 teaspoon cinnamon
1 teaspoon salt
¼ teaspoon freshly ground black
   pepper
½ cup butter
½ teaspoon ground saffron,
   dissolved in 2 tablespoons hot
   water

Loubia Polo

1. Clean and wash 3 cups of rice 5 times in cold water. It is then desirable but not essential to soak the rice in 8 cups of water with 2 tablespoons of salt for at least 2 hours.

2. In a saucepan, brown the onion and meat in 3 tablespoons oil. Add tomatoes, paste and ½ cup hot water. Cover and simmer 20 minutes. Add green beans, cinnamon, 1 teaspoon salt and ¼ teaspoon pepper. Cover and simmer 30 minutes longer over low heat.

3. Bring 8 cups water and 2 tablespoons salt to a boil in a large non-stick pot. Pour the washed and drained rice into the pot. Boil briskly for 6 minutes, stirring gently twice to loosen any grains that may have stuck to the bottom. Drain rice in a colander and rinse in lukewarm water.

4. In the same pot, heat half the butter, 2 tablespoons oil and a drop of dissolved saffron.

5. Place 2 spatulas full of rice in the pan, then add a layer of the green beans and meat mixture. Repeat these steps, arranging the rice in the shape of a pyramid. Pour the remaining butter and saffron over this pyramid.

6. Place a clean dishtowel or paper towel over the pot and cover firmly with lid to prevent steam from escaping. Cook 10 minutes over medium heat and 50 minutes over low heat. Remove from heat and allow to cool for 5 minutes on a damp surface without opening.

7. Lift lid, remove 2 tablespoons of saffron-flavored rice and set aside for use as garnish.

8. Then, gently taking one skimmer or spatula full of rice at a time, place it in an oval serving platter without disturbing the crust. Mound the rice in the shape of a cone and garnish with saffron-flavored rice.

9. Detach the bottom layer using a wooden spatula. Unmold onto a small platter and serve on the side.

Rice with Meat Brochettes

Chelo Kabab

Chelo kabab is Iran's national dish, the equivalent of meat and potatoes in America. It is eaten in every household, regardless of social class; it can be found everywhere, from palaces to stalls in the bazaar. But the best *chelo kababs* are probably those sold in the bazaars.

Foreign visitors enjoy this dish as much as we do. They are always astonished to see the vendor grab the red-hot skewer from the coals and transfer the meat to the plate with only a piece of bread to protect his hands.

Chelo kabab consists of the *chelo* (steamed rice, page 95) and *kabab* (page 89), brochettes of marinated lamb, veal or beef cubes or ground meat and grilled tomatoes. The traditional way to serve *chelo kabab* is as follows:

—Heap a pyramid of *chelo* on each plate. Make a small well in the center of the pyramid and drop an egg yolk into it. Add a dab of butter and sprinkle with a teaspoon of powdered sumac. Mix well.

—Place the *kababs* (*kabab-e kubideh, kabab-e barg* or both) and the grilled tomatoes on the rice. Cover with an opened pita bread to keep everything warm.

—Serve hot with *sabzi-khordan* (fresh herbs and scallions, page 8)), *mast-o khiar* (yogurt and cucumber, page 12), *mast-o musir* (yogurt and shallots, page 13), and *torshi* (Persian pickles, page 164). *Chelo kabab* is often washed down with *doogh* (page 230), a yogurt drink with mint. See page 89 for *kabab-e kubideh* (ground meat brochettes), page 73 for *kabab-e barg* (lamb brochettes), and page 95 for *chelo* (plain rice).

The prudent housewife should always keep some meat marinating in the refrigerator at home to serve to unexpected guests and hungry members of the family. Then while the *chelo* rice is cooking, the fire can be started and the brochettes prepared. This is truly convenience cooking.

Ground Meat and Lamb Brochettes
Kabab-e Kubideh-o Kabab-e Barg
pages 89, 73

Rice with Green Beans
Loubia Polo
page 118

Oven-Baked Rice
Shirazy Polo
page 98

Rice with Fresh Herbs and Fish accompanied with Bitter Lemon,
Lavash Bread, Golden Rice Crust, Herb Kookoo and Persian Pickles
Sabzi Polo ba Mahi va Narenj, Nan-e Lavash, Tah Digue, Kookoo-ye Sabzi va Torshi
page 126

Rice with Tomato Sauce

Makes 6 servings
Preparation time: 50 min. plus 2 hrs. soaking time (optional)
Cooking time: 1 hr.

اسلامبولی پلو

Eslamboli Polo

1 onion, finely chopped
2 pounds stewing meat of lamb, veal or beef, cut in ½-inch cubes
4 tablespoons oil
3 tablespoons tomato paste
3 large tomatoes, peeled and sliced

¼ teaspoon turmeric
½ teaspoon ground cinnamon
1 teaspoon salt
¼ teaspoon freshly ground black pepper
3 cups long-grain rice
½ cup butter

1. Clean and wash 3 cups of rice 5 times in cold water. It is then desirable but not essential to soak the rice in 8 cups of water with 2 tablespoons of salt for at least 2 hours.

2. In a deep saucepan, brown the onion and the meat in 4 tablespoons oil. Add tomato paste and tomatoes, 1 cup water, turmeric, cinnamon and 1 teaspoon salt and ¼ teaspoon pepper. Cover and simmer over low heat for about 40 minutes.

3. Bring 8 cups water and 2 tablespoons salt to a boil in a large, non-stick pot. Pour the washed and drained rice into the pot. Boil briskly for 6 minutes, stirring gently twice to loosen any grains that may have stuck to the bottom. Drain rice in a colander and rinse in lukewarm water.

4. In the same pot, heat half the butter.

5. Place 2 spatulas full of rice in the pot, then add a large spoonful of the meat mixture. Continue to alternate layers of rice and meat until all the ingredients are used up. Arrange the rice in the shape of a pyramid and pour remaining butter over it.

6. Place a clean dishtowel or paper towel over the pot and cover firmly with lid to prevent steam from escaping. Cook 10 minutes over high heat and 50 minutes over low heat. Remove from heat and allow to cool for 5 minutes on a damp surface without opening.

7. Gently taking one skimmer or spatula full of rice at a time, place it in an oval serving platter without disturbing the crust. Mound the rice in the shape of a cone.

8. Detach the bottom layer using a wooden spatula. Unmold onto a small platter and serve on the side.

9. Serve immediately with *torshi* (Persian pickles, page 164) and *sabzi-khordan* (fresh vegetables and herbs, page 8).

Rice with Spinach

Makes 6 servings
Preparation time: 1 hr. 30 min.
plus 2 hrs. marinating
Cooking time: 1 hr. 30 min.

3 cups long-grain rice
2 cups yogurt
2 egg yolks
½ teaspoon saffron, dissolved in
    ¼ cup hot water
2 onions, chopped
2 cloves garlic, crushed
1 teaspoon salt
¼ teaspoon freshly ground black
    pepper

3 pounds boned leg of lamb,
    cut in pieces
2 pounds fresh or 2 packages
    frozen chopped spinach
⅔ cup butter or oil
2 cups pitted prunes or dried
    apricots

Tah Chin-e Esfenaj

1. Clean and wash 3 cups of rice 5 times in cold water. It is then desirable but not essential to soak the rice in 8 cups of water with 2 tablespoons of salt for at least 2 hours.

2. In a bowl, combine the yogurt with the egg, half the dissolved saffron, 1 onion, the garlic, 1 teaspoon salt and ¼ teaspoon pepper. Marinate the meat in this sauce for at least 2 hours.

3. Remove the meat from the yogurt sauce, saving the sauce. Cover and bake the meat in a preheated 350°F oven for 1 hour.

4. Chop the cleaned and washed spinach into large pieces. Steam the spinach in a steamer for 10 minutes and set aside.

5. Brown the one onion in 3 tablespoons butter, add the spinach and prunes and simmer for 3 minutes over low heat.

6. Bring 8 cups water and 2 tablespoons salt to a boil in a large non-stick pot. Pour the washed and drained rice into the pot. Boil briskly for 6 minutes, stirring gently twice to loosen any grains that may have stuck to the bottom. Drain rice in a colander and rinse in lukewarm water.

7. In a bowl, combine 2 skimmers full of rice with the egg, yogurt and half the remaining dissolved saffron.

8. Pour half the remaining butter into a deep ovenproof baking dish with a cover and add the mixture of rice and yogurt. Place the pieces of meat on top and add a layer of spinach and prunes. Cover with rice. Pour the remaining saffron and butter and meat juices over the rice. Pack firmly with a wooden spoon and cover.

9. Place baking dish in a preheated 350°F oven and bake for 90 minutes.

10. Remove baking dish from oven. To unmold, first allow to cool on a damp surface for 10 minutes. Then loosen the rice around the edge of the baking dish with the point of a knife. Place a large serving dish over the baking dish. Hold both dishes firmly with your hands and turn upside down.

11. Serve hot.

Rice with Lamb

Makes 6 servings
Preparation time: 1 hr. 10 min.
plus 2 hrs. marinating
Cooking time: 1 hr. 30 min.

2 egg yolks
1 teaspoon ground saffron, dissolved in 2 tablespoons hot water
1 tablespoon slivered orange peel, boiled in 3 changes of water and drained
1 onion, chopped
2 cloves garlic, crushed

1 teaspoon salt
¼ teaspoon freshly ground black pepper
3 pounds boned leg of lamb or large fryer chicken
3 cups long-grain rice
⅔ cup butter

Tah Chin-e Barreh

1. In a bowl, combine the yogurt with the egg yolks, half the dissolved saffron, the slivered orange peel, the onion and the garlic. Add 1 teaspoon salt and ¼ teaspoon pepper to taste and marinate meat in this sauce for at least 2 hours and up to 24 hours.

2. Clean and wash 3 cups of rice 5 times in cold water. It is then desirable but not essential to soak the rice in 8 cups of water with 2 tablespoons of salt for at least 2 hours.

3. Remove meat from yogurt, reserving yogurt. Cover and bake in preheated 350°F oven for 1 hour.

4. Bring 8 cups water and 2 tablespoons salt to a boil in a large non-stick pot. Pour the washed and drained rice into the pot. Boil briskly for 6 minutes, stirring gently twice to loosen any grains that may have stuck to the bottom. Drain rice in a colander and rinse in lukewarm water.

5. Combine 2 spatulas full of rice with the yogurt sauce.

6. Pour half the melted butter into a deep ovenproof baking dish with a cover and add the mixture of rice and yogurt. Place the pieces of meat on top and cover with the remaining rice. Pour the remaining saffron and butter over the rice. Pack firmly using a wooden spoon and cover.

7. Place baking dish in a preheated 350°F oven and bake 90 minutes.

8. Remove baking dish from oven. To unmold, first allow to cool on a damp surface for 10 minutes. Then loosen the rice around the edges of the baking dish with the point of a knife. Place a large serving dish over the baking dish. Hold both dishes firmly with two hands and turn upside down.

9. Serve hot.

Rice with Fresh Herbs and Fish

Makes 6 servings
Preparation time: 45 min. plus 2
hrs. soaking time (optional)
Cooking time: 1 hr.

3 cups long-grain rice
½ cup chopped chives or scallions
1½ cups coarsely chopped parsley
1½ cups coarsely chopped fresh dill
⅔ cup butter
½ teaspoon ground saffron, dissolved in 2 tablespoons hot water
3 whole cloves garlic, unpeeled

2 whole leeks, washed thoroughly but left whole
1 large white-fleshed fish, like striped bass or sea bass, about 3 pounds
½ cup flour for dredging
4 tablespoons oil
Juice of 2 bitter oranges, if available, or juice of 2 lemons

Sabzi Polo Ba Mahi

1. Clean and wash 3 cups of rice 5 times in cold water. It is then desirable but not essential to soak the rice in 8 cups of water with 2 tablespoons of salt for at least 2 hours.

2. Wash chives, parsley and dill; pat dry and chop.

3. Bring 8 cups water and 2 tablespoons salt to a boil in a large non-stick pot. Pour the washed and drained rice into the pot. Boil briskly for 6 minutes, stirring gently twice to loosen any grains that may have stuck to the bottom. Drain rice in a colander and rinse in lukewarm water.

4. In the same pot, heat half the butter and a drop of dissolved saffron.

5. Place 2 spatulas full of rice in the pot, then add 1 spatula full of herbs, the garlic cloves and leeks. Repeat these steps, arranging the rice in the shape of a pyramid. Pour the remaining butter, half the saffron and 2 tablespoons hot water over this pyramid.

6. Place a clean dishtowel or paper towel over the pot and cover firmly with lid to prevent steam from escaping. Cook 10 minutes over medium heat and 50 minutes over low heat.

7. While the rice is cooking, scale and clean the fish, removing the head, tail and fins. Cut the fish down the center lengthwise, without removing the backbone. Slice across into 6 pieces.

8. Wash fish and pat dry. Dust it in a mixture of flour and salt.

9. Just before serving, brown fish on both sides in 4 tablespoons oil in a skillet over low heat. Add more oil if necessary.

10. Remove saucepan of rice from heat and allow to cool for 5 minutes on a damp surface without opening.

11. Open and remove 2 tablespoons of saffron-flavored rice and set aside for garnishing. Then, gently taking one skimmer or spatula full of rice at a time, place it in an oval serving platter without disturbing the crust. Mound the rice in the shape of a cone. Garnish with the saffroned rice.

12. Detach the bottom layer using a wooden spatula. Unmold onto a small platter and serve on the side.

13. Arrange fish on a serving platter. Garnish with the bitter-orange or lemon juice and the remaining saffron.

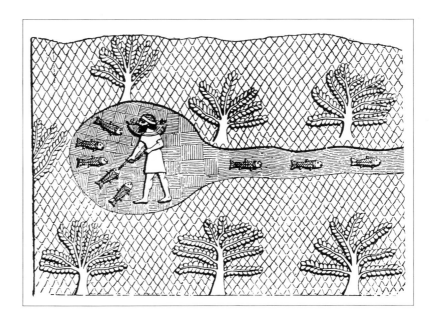

Rice with Apricots

Makes 6 servings
Preparation time: 1 hr. 15 min.
plus 2 hrs. soaking time (optional)
Cooking time: 1 hr.

3 cups long-grain rice
⅔ cup melted butter or oil
2 onions, finely chopped
1½ pounds boned leg or shoulder of lamb, cut in small pieces
1 teaspoon salt
¼ teaspoon freshly ground black pepper

1 teaspoon cinnamon
½ teaspoon ground saffron, dissolved in 2 tablespoons hot water
½ cup raisins
1 cup dried apricots chopped in small pieces
2 tablespoons yogurt

Gheisi Polo

1. Clean and wash 3 cups of rice 5 times in cold water. It is then desirable but not essential to soak the rice in 8 cups of water with 2 tablespoons of salt for at least 2 hours.

2. In a saucepan, saute the finely chopped onions in 3 tablespoons butter; add the meat. Season with 1 teaspoon salt, ¼ teaspoon pepper and cinnamon. Pour in 1 cup water. Cover and simmer 1 hour over low heat. Add a third of the saffron.

3. Wash raisins and apricots and saute in 2 teaspoons butter.

4. Bring 8 cups water and 2 tablespoons salt to a boil in a large non-stick pot. Pour the washed and drained the rice into the pot. Boil briskly for 6 minutes, stirring gently twice to loosen any grains that may have stuck to the bottom. Drain rice in a colander and rinse in lukewarm water.

5. In the same pot, heat 4 teaspoons of the butter, a third of the saffron and the yogurt.

6. Sprinkle 2 spatulas full of rice in the pot. Add a few pieces of meat, 1 spatula full of apricots and the raisins. Repeat, arranging the rice in the shape of a pyramid.

7. Pour the remaining melted butter, the meat juices and the remaining saffron over this pyramid.

8. Place a clean dishtowel or paper towel over the pot and cover firmly with lid to prevent steam from escaping. Cook 10 minutes over medium heat and 50 minutes over low heat. Remove from heat and allow to cool for 5 minutes on a damp surface without opening.

9. Open the pot, take 2 tablespoons of the saffron-flavored rice and set aside for garnishing.

10. Gently taking one skimmer or spatula full of rice at a time, place it in an oval serving platter without disturbing the crust. Mound the rice in the shape of a cone. Decorate with saffron-flavored rice.

11. Detach the bottom layer using a wooden spatula. Unmold onto a small platter and serve on the side.

If a Pot Can Multiply

One day Mulla lent his cooking pots to a neighbor, who was giving a feast. The neighbor returned them, together with an extra one–a very tiny pot.

"What is this?" asked Mulla.

"According to law, I have given you the offspring of your property which was born when the pots were in my care," said the joker.

Shortly afterwards Mulla borrowed his neighbor's pots, but did not return them.

The man came round to get them back.

"Alas!" said Mulla Nasrudin, "they are dead. We have established, have we not, that pots are mortal?"

S T E W S

گر تو افتدم نظر چهره به چهره رو به رو   شرح دهم غم ترا نکته به نکته مو به مو

از پی دیدن رخت بمجو صبا فانم   کوچه به کوچه، در به در، خانه به خانه کو به کو

دور دهان تنگ تو، عارض عنبرین خط   غنچه غنچه، گل به گل، لاله به لاله، بو به بو

می رود از فراق تو خون دل از دو دیده‌ام   دجله به دجله، یم به یم، چشمه چشمه جو به جو

مهر ترا دل خوین بافته بر قماش جان   رشته به رشته نخ به نخ، تار به تار، پو به پو

دسته واقعین

If I see you, face to face, eye to eye
I will tell you of my sadness, point by point, item by item
Like the east wind I search for you
In the streets, door to door, house to house
For your sweet lips, your gentle features
Your fragrance, blossom to blossom, flower to flower
Separated from you my heart bleeds through both eyes
To the sea, spring to spring, river to river
Love for you has woven this afflicted heart
To the stuff of life
Strand to strand, thread to thread

Ghoratalaine

S t e w s

Khoreshe is a delicate stew. It is a combination of either meats (lamb, beef or veal) or poultry or fish with vegetables, fresh or dried fruits, beans, grains and sometimes nuts. It is seasoned subtly with fresh herbs and spices, then simmered for a long time over low heat. To achieve the slow fusing of flavors that characterizes *khoreshe*, it is best to cook it in a heavy pot, cast-iron if possible. I recommend a classic Dutch oven, but any heavy stew pot will do.

Khoreshe can be made in advance and reheated just before serving; in fact, it often improves after sitting for a while.

The good Persian cook always uses whatever vegetables and fruits are in season when preparing *khoreshe*, not only because it is more economical to do so, but because their freshness enhances the flavor of the dish. For every recipe I have simply specified stewing meat. However, for exceptionally good results, use in the case of lamb "the leg or shanks" and for veal or beef the "eye round," carefully monitoring the cooking period.

Khoreshe is always served with rice. *Chelo* (see page 95) is heaped on each dinner plate and the *khoreshe* is served on top of it. In Iran this is called *chelo khoreshe*.

Okra Stew

Makes 6 servings
Preparation time: 30 min.
Cooking time: 1 hr. 40 min.

2 onions, finely sliced
2 cloves garlic, crushed
3 tablespoons oil
1 pound stewing meat, lamb, veal or beef, cut into 1-inch cubes
1¼ teaspoons salt
¼ teaspoon freshly ground black pepper

1 teaspoon turmeric
3 tablespoons tomato paste or 4 tomatoes, peeled and sliced
½ red pepper, chopped (optional)
1 pound fresh or frozen okra
½ cup pitted dates, chopped (optional)
Juice of 1 lemon

Khoresh-e Bamieh

1. In a Dutch oven, brown onions and garlic in 3 tablespoons oil. Add pieces of meat and brown. Sprinkle with salt, pepper and turmeric. Add tomato paste or tomatoes and red pepper. Stir in 3 cups water. Cover and simmer for 1 hour 15 minutes over low heat.

2. While meat is cooking, wash okra and cut off stems. Boil it in salted water for 10 minutes and drain.

3. When the meat is done, add pitted dates, lemon juice and okra. Simmer, uncovered, for 15 minutes over low heat. Check to see if meat and okra are cooked. Taste sauce and adjust seasoning.

4. Transfer stew to a deep casserole dish. Cover and place in a warm oven until serving time. Serve hot with *chelo* rice (page 95).

Mushroom Stew

Makes 6 servings
Preparation time: 30 min.
Cooking time: 1 hr. 35 min.

1 fryer chicken, about 3 pounds, or 1 pound stewing meat, veal, lamb or beef, cut in 1-inch cubes
2 onions, finely sliced
2 cloves of garlic, crushed
5 tablespoons oil
½ teaspoon salt
¼ teaspoon freshly ground black pepper

1 pound fresh mushrooms
1 tablespoon flour
2 tablespoons chopped parsley
2 tablespoons lemon juice
¼ teaspoon ground saffron, dissolved in 1 tablespoon hot water
2 egg yolks

Khoresh-e Gharche

1. Cut the chicken into 6 pieces. Rinse and drain.

2. In a Dutch oven, brown onions and garlic and saute the meat or chicken in 3 tablespoons oil. Add salt and pepper. Pour in water—1 cup for chicken, 2½ cups for meat. Cover and simmer over low heat for about 55 minutes for meat and 30 minutes for chicken, stirring occasionally.

3. Clean mushrooms, cut off stems and slice. Sprinkle with flour and saute in 2 tablespoons oil. Add parsley.

4. When the chicken or meat is done, add mushrooms, lemon juice and saffron. Cover and simmer 35 minutes over low heat.

5. Check to see that chicken or meat is cooked. Taste sauce and adjust seasoning. Add beaten egg yolks. Simmer 5 minutes over low heat, gently stirring.

6. Transfer to a flameproof casserole dish. Cover and place in warm oven until ready to serve. Serve hot from same dish with *chelo* (page 95).

Carrot and Prune Stew

Makes 6 servings
Preparation time: 20 min.
Cooking time: 1 hr. 40 min.

2 onions, finely sliced
1 clove garlic, crushed
⅓ cup oil or butter
1 fryer chicken, about 3 pounds, cut in 6 pieces, or 1 pound stewing meat, lamb, veal or beef, cut in 1-inch cubes
1 teaspoon salt
¼ teaspoon freshly ground black pepper
1 teaspoon cinnamon

¼ teaspoon turmeric
¼ teaspoon ground cardamom (optional)
1 pound carrots scraped and sliced
¼ teaspoon of saffron, dissolved in 1 tablespoon hot water
½ cup orange juice
2 cups pitted prunes

Khoresh-e Havij-o Alou

1. Brown the onions and garlic in 3 tablespoons oil. Add the chicken or meat and brown the pieces. Stir in the salt, pepper, cinnamon, turmeric and cardamom. Add water—1½ cups for chicken, 2½ cups for meat. Cover and simmer over low heat for 30 minutes for chicken and 1 hour for meat.

2. Saute the carrots in 2 tablespoons oil and add to the chicken or meat. Add dissolved saffron and orange juice. Cover and simmer for 25 minutes over low heat. Add prunes and let simmer for 15 minutes longer.

3. Check to be sure chicken or meat and carrots are cooked. Taste sauce and correct seasoning. Transfer to a deep ovenproof casserole dish, cover and place in warm oven until ready to serve.

4. Serve hot with *chelo* (page 95).

Pumpkin and Prune Stew

Makes 6 servings
Preparation time: 35 min.
Cooking time: 1 hr. 25 min.

2 onions, finely sliced
1 pound stewing meat with ½ pound marrow bone, lamb, veal or beef, cut in 1-inch cubes, or 1 fryer chicken, about 3 pounds, cut into pieces
⅓ cup oil or butter
1 teaspoon salt
¼ teaspoon freshly ground black pepper

1 teaspoon ground cinnamon
2 pounds fresh pumpkin
2 tablespoons sugar (optional)
¼ cup lemon juice
¼ teaspoon saffron, dissolved in 1 tablespoon hot water
2 cups pitted prunes

Khoresh-e Kadou Halvai-o Alou

1. In a Dutch oven, brown onions and saute the meat, including bone, or chicken in 3 tablespoons oil. Add salt, pepper and cinnamon. Pour in 2½ cups water for meat or 1½ cups for chicken. Cover and cook over low heat for about 55 minutes for meat and 35 minutes for chicken, stirring occasionally.

2. Meanwhile, peel and cut pumpkin flesh into 2-inch cubes. Brown them in a skillet on both sides in the remaining oil. Set aside.

3. When the chicken is done, add the sugar, lemon juice, saffron, prunes and pumpkin pieces. Cover and simmer 30 minutes longer over low heat.

4. Check that meat or chicken and pumpkin are cooked. Taste sauce and adjust seasoning.

5. In a deep casserole dish, carefully arrange first the pumpkin pieces, then the meat and sauce. Cover and place in a warm oven until ready to serve. Serve from the same dish with *chelo* (page 95).

Cardoon Stew

Makes 6 servings
Preparation time: 35 min.
Cooking time: 1 hr. 30 min.

Khoresh-e Kangar

2 fresh cardoon stalks, about 1
  pound or frozen package
1 teaspoon vinegar
2 onions, finely sliced
1 pound stewing meat with ½
  pound marrow bone, lamb,
  veal or beef; cut meat into
  1-inch cubes
⅓ cup oil
1 teaspoon salt
¼ teaspoon freshly ground black
  pepper

¼ teaspoon turmeric
1 teaspoon *advieh* (allspice, page
  160)
¼ teaspoon saffron, dissolved in
  1 tablespoon hot water
4 tablespoons lemon juice or ½
  cup *ab goureh* (sour grape juice)
1 tablespoon tomato paste

1. Carefully remove and discard prickly parts of cardoons after removing leafy heads. Be sure to remove strings by lifting them with the tip of a knife and peeling them off. Cut into pieces 2 inches long. To prevent the vegetable from discoloring and to keep it tender, soak pieces of peeled cardoon in a bowl of water with a splash of vinegar until ready to use. If using frozen cardoon, there is no need for soaking in water.

2. In a Dutch oven, brown onions and meat, including bone, in 3 tablespoons oil. Add salt, pepper, turmeric and *advieh*. Pour in 2½ cups water. Cover and simmer for about 30 minutes over low heat, stirring occasionally.

3. Drain cardoon and in a skillet, brown pieces in remaining oil.

4. When the meat is done, add dissolved saffron, lemon juice, tomato paste and the cardoon. Cover and simmer for 1 hour over low heat.

5. Check to be sure meat and cardoons are cooked. Taste and correct seasoning. Transfer to a deep casserole dish, cover and place in a warm oven until ready to serve.

6. Serve hot from the same dish with *chelo* (page 95).

Note: *Ab goureh* (sour grape juice) and *advieh* are available at food specialty shops (page 240).

Celery Stew

Makes 6 servings
Preparation time: 30 min.
Cooking time: 1 hr. 30 min.

2 onions, finely sliced
1 pound stewing meat with ½ pound marrow bones, lamb veal or beef; cut meat into 1-inch cubes
⅓ cup oil or butter
1 teaspoon salt
¼ teaspoon freshly ground black pepper
½ teaspoon turmeric
1 bunch celery (4 cups, chopped)
1 cup chopped parsley

3 sprigs of mint, chopped or 1 tablespoon dried mint
⅓ cup fresh lemon juice or ½ cup *ab goureh* (sour grape juice) or 1 cup *gojeh sabz* (unripe plums)
¼ teaspoon ground saffron, dissolved in 1 tablespoon hot water
½ tablespoon tomato paste or 2 fresh tomatoes, peeled and sliced (optional)

Khoresh-e Karafse

1. In a Dutch oven, brown onions and meat, including bone, in 3 tablespoons oil. Add salt, pepper and turmeric. Pour in 2½ cups water, cover and simmer for about 1 hour over low heat.

2. Wash celery and cut into 1-inch pieces. Brown celery and saute parsley and mint in the remaining oil.

3. When the meat is done, add the mixture of celery and herbs, the lemon juice, dissolved saffron and the tomato paste or tomatoes. Cover and simmer 30 minutes longer.

4. Check that meat is cooked. Taste and adjust seasoning. Transfer to a deep casserole dish, cover and place in warm oven until time to serve.

5. Serve hot, from the same dish, with *chelo* (page 95).

Note: *Ab goureh* (sour grape juice) and *gojeh sabz* (unripe plums) are available at Middle Eastern food shops (page 240).

Green Bean Stew

Makes 6 servings
Preparation time: 30 min.
Cooking time: 1 hr. 30 min.

2 onions, finely sliced
1 pound stewing meat, veal, lamb or beef, cut in 1-inch cubes
⅓ cup oil or butter
1 teaspoon salt
¼ teaspoon freshly ground black pepper
½ teaspoon cinnamon

¼ teaspoon turmeric
¼ teaspoon ground nutmeg
1 pound fresh or frozen green beans
2 tablespoons lemon juice
3 tablespoons tomato paste or 5 medium tomatoes, peeled and sliced

Khoresh-e Loubia Sabz

1. Brown onions and meat in 3 tablespoons oil in a Dutch oven. Add salt, pepper, cinnamon, turmeric and nutmeg. Pour in 2½ cups water. Cover and cook for about 45 minutes over low heat, stirring occasionally.

2. Remove strings, if any, from beans. Cut into 1-inch pieces. Wash and drain. Saute in a skillet in 2 tablespoons oil.

3. When meat is done, add green beans. Add lemon juice and tomato paste or tomatoes. Cover and simmer 45 minutes longer over low heat.

4. Check to see that meat is cooked. Taste and correct seasoning. Transfer to an ovenproof casserole dish, cover and place in warm oven until ready to serve.

5. Serve hot from the same dish with *chelo* (page 95).

Spinach and Prune Stew

Makes 6 servings
Preparation time: 20 min.
Cooking time: 1 hr. 30 min.

2 onions, finely sliced
⅓ cup oil or butter
1 pound stewing meat with ½ pound marrow bone, lamb, veal or beef; cut meat into 1-inch cubes
1½ teaspoons salt
¼ teaspoon freshly ground black pepper
1 teaspoon cinnamon

¼ teaspoon turmeric
1 pound washed and coarsely chopped spinach or 1 package frozen chopped spinach
2 cups chopped chives or scallions
3 tablespoons *ab goureh* (sour grape juice) or lemon juice
2 cups pitted prunes

Khoresh-e Esfenaj-o Alou

1. In a Dutch oven, brown onions in 3 tablespoons oil. Add meat, including bone, and brown. Add salt, pepper, cinnamon and turmeric. Pour in 2½ cups water and bring to a boil. Cover and simmer 45 minutes over low heat.

2. In a skillet saute spinach and chives for 3 minutes in the rest of the oil.

3. When the meat is done, add spinach, chives and sour grape juice or lemon juice. Cover and simmer 30 minutes more over medium heat.

4. Add prunes to stew, cover and let simmer for 15 minutes more.

5. Check to see that meat is cooked. Taste sauce and adjust seasoning. Transfer stew to a deep casserole dish. Cover and place in warm oven until ready to serve.

6. Serve hot from the same dish with *chelo* (page 95).

Note: *Ab goureh* (sour grape juice) is available at Middle Eastern food shops (page 240).

Pomegranate Stew

Makes 6 servings
Preparation time: 30 min.
Cooking time: 2 hrs.

2 large onions, chopped
2 cloves garlic, crushed
3 tablespoons oil
1⅓ cups ground walnuts
1 teaspoon salt
¼ teaspoon freshly ground black pepper
½ teaspoon cinnamon
½ teaspoon nutmeg
1 cup fresh orange juice

5 tablespoons pomegranate paste or 2 cups fresh pomegranate juice
3 teaspoons sugar
¼ teaspoon saffron, dissolved in 1 tablespoon hot water
1 large fryer or duck, 4–5 pounds, cut up

Khoresh-e Fessenjan

1. Brown one onion and garlic in 3 tablespoons oil in Dutch oven. Add ground walnuts and saute 3 minutes, stirring constantly. Mix in the salt, pepper, cinnamon and nutmeg. Pour in 1½ cups water.

2. Combine orange juice, pomegranate paste or juice, sugar and dissolved saffron. Add to onions and nuts; cover and simmer 20 minutes over low heat, stirring occasionally. (Add more sugar to taste if pomegranate paste is too sour.)

3. In a pot, place one chopped onion and the chicken or duck pieces (do not add water). Cover and simmer over low heat, 30 minutes for chicken, 1 hour for duck. Remove unnecessary bones and the skin from the chicken or duck.

4. Place the chicken or duck in the Dutch oven with the pomegranate sauce. Cover and simmer over low heat for 30 minutes longer for chicken, 1 hour for duck, stirring gently occasionally.

5. Check to see if chicken or duck is done; taste sauce and adjust seasoning. Transfer to a deep ovenproof casserole dish, cover and place in warm oven until ready to serve.

6. Serve hot from the same dish with *chelo* (page 95).

Variation: This stew can be made with meatballs instead of poultry. Knead 1 grated onion into 1 pound ground meat and shape into meatballs the size of hazelnuts. Brown them on all sides in oil and add in step 4. Continue as in master recipe, cooking for 30 minutes.

Pomegranate and Herb Stew

Makes 6 servings
Preparation time: 30 min.
Cooking time: 1 hr. 50 min.

Khoresh-e Anar Avij

1 chicken, about 3 pounds, or 1 pound stewing meat, veal, lamb or beef, cut into 1-inch pieces
2 onions, thinly sliced
3 cloves garlic, crushed
⅓ cup oil or butter
1 cup chopped scallions
1 cup chopped fresh coriander leaves or ½ cup dried leaves
½ cup chopped fresh mint or ¼ cup dried mint
1 cup chopped parsley

1 teaspoon salt
¼ teaspoon pepper
¼ teaspoon cinnamon
1 cup finely ground walnuts
2½ cups pomegranate juice or ½ cup pomegranate
2 tablespoons rice flour (ground rice) dissolved in 1½ cups of water for chicken or 2½ cups water for meat
2 eggs, beaten
2 tablespoons sugar (see note)

1. Cut chicken into 6 pieces; rinse and drain.

2. In a Dutch oven, brown onions and garlic in 3 tablespoons of oil or butter. Add the chopped herbs, salt, pepper, cinnamon and walnuts. Pour in pomegranate juice or diluted paste.

3. Add dissolved rice flour and stir in. Cover and simmer 20 minutes over low heat, stirring occasionally.

4. In a skillet, brown chicken pieces or meat in remaining oil or butter. Add to Dutch oven. Cover and simmer over low heat 1 hour for chicken, 1½ hours for meat.

5. Check to see that chicken or meat is done; taste sauce and correct seasoning. Stir in eggs.

6. Transfer stew to a deep casserole dish, cover and place in warm oven until serving time. Serve with *chelo* (page 95).

Variation: This stew may be made with tiny meatballs. Knead 1 grated onion into 1 pound ground meat and form into balls the size of hazelnuts. Brown in oil and add to Dutch oven instead of chicken in step 4.

Note: If the pomegranate paste is too sour, add sugar.

Spinach and Orange Stew

Makes 6 servings
Preparation time: 30 min.
Cooking time: 1 hr.

1 pound ground lamb, veal or beef
1 onion, grated
1 teaspoon salt
¼ teaspoon freshly ground black pepper
⅓ cup oil or butter
1 pound fresh or frozen chopped spinach
1 cup chopped parsley

2 cloves garlic, crushed
¼ teaspoon turmeric
1 cup fresh orange juice
2 tablespoons fresh lemon juice
1 tablespoon flour
¼ teaspoon ground saffron dissolved in 1 tablespoon hot water

Khoresh-e Saak

1. Combine the meat, grated onion, ½ teaspoon salt and a pinch of pepper in a bowl. Shape into small meatballs the size of a hazelnut. Brown in a skillet in 2 tablespoons oil or butter.

2. In a Dutch oven, saute spinach, parsley and crushed garlic in remaining oil or butter. Stir in ½ teaspoon salt, ¼ teaspoon pepper and the turmeric. Add 1 cup water and the meatballs. Cover and cook for about 30 minutes over low heat.

3. In a bowl, combine orange juice, lemon juice, flour and saffron. Add this mixture to Dutch oven. Cover and simmer 30 minutes longer over low heat.

4. Check that stew is done; taste sauce and correct seasoning. Transfer to deep ovenproof casserole dish; cover and place in warm oven until ready to serve.

5. Serve hot from same dish with *chelo* (page 95).

Orange Stew

Makes 6 servings
Preparation time: 30 min.
Cooking time: 1 hr. 20 min.

1 fryer chicken, about 3 pounds
2 onions, finely sliced
⅓ cup oil or butter
2 tablespoons shredded orange peel (see note)
1 teaspoon salt
¼ teaspoon pepper
1 teaspoon cinnamon
2 carrots
¼ teaspoon ground saffron, dissolved in 1 tablespoon hot water

2 tablespoons sugar
¼ cup lemon juice or vinegar
1 tablespoon flour
4 oranges

GARNISH
2 teaspoons slivered pistachio nuts
2 teaspoons slivered almonds

Khoresh-e Porteghal

1. Cut chicken into 6 pieces. Rinse and drain.

2. In a Dutch oven, brown onions and chicken pieces in 3 tablespoons oil. Add orange peel, salt, pepper and cinnamon. Pour in 1½ cups water, cover and simmer for 35 minutes.

3. Scrape the carrots and slice into thin slivers. Saute in 2 tablespoons butter. Add it to the chicken and simmer for 15 minutes.

4. In a bowl, combine the saffron, sugar, lemon juice or vinegar and flour. Mix well.

5. When the chicken is done, add the mixture of lemon juice or vinegar, saffron, sugar and flour. Cover and simmer for 15 minutes.

6. Peel the oranges, separate into segments and peel skin from each segment. Add to Dutch oven, uncover and simmer for 15 minutes to allow the pieces of orange to absorb the sauce.

7. Check to see that chicken is cooked. Taste and adjust seasoning. Add more sugar or lemon juice to your taste. Transfer to a deep ovenproof casserole dish. Cover and place in warm oven until ready to serve.

8. Just before serving, sprinkle with slivered pistachio nuts and almonds. Serve hot from the same dish with *chelo* (page 95).

Note: If fresh orange peel is used, place slivered orange peel in a pan and cover with water, bring to a boil and drain, to remove bitterness.

Variation: 1. Canned orange segments or tangerines may be substituted for fresh orange and orange peel. 2. This dish may also be made without carrots.

Rhubarb Stew

Makes 6 servings
Preparation time: 30 min.
Cooking time: 1 hr. 40 min.

2 onions, finely sliced
1 pound stewing meat with ½ pound marrow bone, lamb, veal or beef; cut meat into 1-inch cubes
⅓ cup oil or butter
1½ teaspoons salt
¼ teaspoon freshly ground black pepper
¼ teaspoon turmeric
1 cup chopped parsley
3 sprigs fresh mint, chopped or 1 tablespoon dried mint
¼ teaspoon ground saffron, dissolved in 1 tablespoon hot water
1 pound fresh or frozen rhubarb

Khoresh-e Rivasse

1. In a Dutch oven, brown onions and meat, including bone, in 3 tablespoons oil or butter. Add salt, pepper and turmeric. Pour in 2½ cups water. Cover and cook for about 1 hour over low heat, stirring occasionally.

2. Saute parsley and mint in a skillet in remaining oil or butter.

3. When meat is done, add parsley and mint, dissolved saffron and lemon juice. Cover and simmer 30 minutes longer over low heat.

4. Remove strings from rhubarb. Wash and cut into 1-inch pieces.

5. Shortly before serving, when the meat is cooked, add rhubarb to meat. Simmer uncovered for 5–10 minutes longer.

6. Check to be sure that meat and rhubarb are done. The rhubarb should not be falling apart. Taste and adjust seasoning. Transfer to a deep ovenproof casserole dish cover and place in warm oven until serving time.

7. Serve hot from same dish with *chelo* (page 95).

Peach Stew

Makes 6 servings
Preparation time: 30 min.
Cooking time: 1 hr. 40 min.

2 onions, finely sliced
1 pound stewing meat, lamb, veal or beef, cut in 1-inch cubes or 1 chicken, about 3 pounds, cut in 6 pieces
⅓ cup oil or butter
1 teaspoon salt
¼ teaspoon freshly ground black pepper

¼ teaspoon cinnamon
¼ cup lemon juice
1 tablespoon flour
½ cup sugar
¼ teaspoon ground saffron dissolved in 1 tablespoon hot water
5 firm unripe peaches

Khoresh-e Houlou

1. Brown onions and meat or chicken in 3 tablespoons oil in a Dutch oven. Add salt, pepper and cinnamon. Pour in water—2½ cups for meat, 1½ cups for chicken. Cover and simmer over low heat for about 30 minutes for chicken and 1 hour for meat.

2. Mix together the lemon juice, flour, sugar and saffron. When the meat is done, stir in the lemon mixture. Cover and simmer 20 minutes longer over low heat.

3. Wash peaches well and cut into ½-inch slices. Saute in a skillet in 2 tablespoons oil. Add to the Dutch oven, cover and simmer 20 minutes longer.

4. Check to see that meat or chicken and peaches are cooked. Taste and correct seasoning. Transfer to a deep ovenproof casserole dish. Cover and place in oven until ready to serve.

5. Serve hot from the same dish with *chelo* (page 95).

Variation: 2 cups sliced peaches in heavy syrup may be substituted for fresh peaches. Just eliminate the sugar and add peaches in the last 10 minutes of cooking.

Quince Stew

Makes 6 servings
Preparation time: 20 min.
Cooking time: 1 hr. 35 min.

2 onions, finely sliced
⅓ cup oil or butter
1 pound stewing meat, lamb,
    veal or beef, cut in 1-inch cubes
1 teaspoon salt
¼ teaspoon pepper
½ teaspoon ground cinnamon
2 large quinces

2 tablespoons sugar
¼ cup vinegar or lemon juice
¼ teaspoon ground saffron
    dissolved in 1 tablespoon hot
    water
⅓ cup yellow split peas

Khoresh-e Beh

1. In a Dutch oven, brown onions in 3 tablespoons oil. Add pieces of meat and brown. Season with salt, pepper, turmeric and cinnamon. Stir in 3 cups water. Cover and simmer over low heat for 1 hour, stirring occasionally.

2. Wash but do not peel quinces. Remove seeds using an apple corer and slice as for apple pie.

3. Saute fruit in 2 tablespoons oil in a skillet. Set aside.

4. When the meat is done, add sugar, vinegar, saffron, split peas and quince. Cover and simmer for 35 minutes.

5. Check to see that meat and fruit are cooked. Taste sauce and correct seasoning. Transfer to a deep ovenproof casserole dish. Cover and place in warm oven until ready to serve.

6. Serve hot from the same dish with *chelo* (page 95).

Apple Stew

Makes 6 servings
Preparation time: 20 min.
Cooking time: 1 hr. 35 min.

1 fryer chicken, about 3 pounds, or 1 pound stewing meat, lamb, veal or beef, cut in 1-inch cubes
2 onions, finely sliced
⅓ cup oil or butter
1 teaspoon salt
¼ teaspoon freshly ground black pepper
½ teaspoon cinnamon

¼ cup yellow split peas
2 tablespoons sugar
2 tablespoons lemon juice or vinegar
¼ teaspoon ground saffron dissolved in 1 tablespoon hot water
5 tart cooking apples

Khoresh-e Sib

1. Cut the chicken into 6 pieces; rinse and drain.

2. In a Dutch oven, brown the onions and saute the chicken or meat in 3 table-spoons oil. Sprinkle with salt, pepper and cinnamon. Add water, 1 cup for chicken and 3 cups for meat. Cover and simmer 30 minutes for chicken and 55 minutes for meat over low heat.

3. Add yellow split peas, tomato paste, sugar, lemon juice or vinegar and saffron. Cover and simmer for 30 minutes longer.

4. Peel and core the apples and cut into wedges as for apple pie. Saute in remaining oil and add to the Dutch oven. Cover and simmer 5 or more minutes longer.

5. Check to see if chicken or meat is done. Taste sauce and correct seasoning, adding more sugar or vinegar if necessary.

6. Transfer stew to a deep casserole dish and place in warm oven until ready to serve. Serve from the same dish with *chelo* (page 95).

Sweet and Sour Chicken Stew

Makes 6 servings
Preparation time: 20 min.
Cooking time: 1 hr.

1 fryer chicken, about 3 pounds
1 onion, chopped
3 cloves garlic, crushed
⅓ cup oil or butter
1 teaspoon salt
¼ teaspoon freshly ground black pepper
1 cup chopped scallions
1 cup chopped parsley
1 cup chopped fresh coriander

½ cup chopped fresh mint
2 tablespoons rice flour (ground rice)
1 cup fresh orange juice, 1 cup bitter-orange juice or ¼ cup fresh lemon juice
2 tablespoons yellow split peas
4 eggs

Khoresh-e Morgh-e Torshe

1. Cut chicken into pieces; rinse and dry. Brown with onion and garlic in 3 tablespoons oil in Dutch oven. Season with salt and pepper. Add 2 cups water. Cover and let simmer over low heat for 30 minutes.

2. Saute scallions, parsley, coriander and mint in remaining oil. Dissolve rice flour in orange juice.

3. Add the yellow split peas, sauteed herbs and orange juice mixture to the chicken. Cover and simmer for 30 minutes longer.

4. Check to see that chicken is done. Taste sauce and adjust seasoning. Transfer to a deep ovenproof casserole dish. Cover and place in warm oven until ready to serve.

5. Just before serving, beat the eggs in a bowl and add to stew, stirring constantly. Serve immediately from same dish with *chelo* (page 95).

Note: Bitter oranges are not always available. Lemon or orange juice may be substituted, though the flavor will be somewhat different.

Fresh Herb Stew

Makes 6 servings
Preparation time: 25 min.
Cooking time: 2 hrs.

2 onions, finely sliced
2 pounds lamb, veal or beef shank
⅓ cup oil
⅓ cup dried kidney beans
1½ teaspoons salt
¼ teaspoon pepper
¼ teaspoon turmeric
2 cups chopped parsley

1 cup chopped chives or scallions
½ cup chopped spinach
3 tablespoons dried fenugreek leaves or ½ cup chopped fresh fenugreek leaves
4 whole *limou-omani*, pierced, or 4 tablespoons lemon juice

Khoresh-e Ghormeh Sabzi

1. Brown onions and meat in 3 tablespoons oil in a Dutch oven. Add kidney beans. Stir in salt, pepper, and turmeric. Pour in 3½ cups water. Bring to a boil, cover and simmer for about 1 hour over low heat, stirring occasionally.

2. Meanwhile, saute the chopped parsley, chives, spinach and fenugreek leaves in the remaining oil for 10 minutes.

3. When the meat and kidney beans are done, add the sauteed herbs and the *limou-omani* or lemon juice. Cover and simmer 1 hour longer over medium heat.

4. Check to see that meat is cooked. Taste and adjust seasoning to your taste. Transfer to a deep ovenproof casserole dish; cover and place in warm oven until ready to serve.

5. Serve hot from same dish with *chelo* (page 95).

Note: Fenugreek leaves and *limou-omani* (dried Persian limes) are available at Middle Eastern food shops (page 240).

Eggplant Stew

Makes 6 servings
Preparation time: 20 min.
Cooking time: 1 hr. 45 min.

خورش بادمجان

Khoresh-e
Bademjan

1 pound stewing meat with ½ pound marrow bone, lamb, veal or beef; cut meat into 1-inch cubes, or a 3-pound fryer chicken, cut up
2 onions, finely sliced
1 clove garlic, crushed
½ cup oil
¼ teaspoon nutmeg
1 teaspoon cinnamon
¼ teaspoon turmeric

1 teaspoon salt
¼ teaspoon freshly ground black pepper
2 medium eggplants
2 tablespoons tomato paste and 1 large tomato, peeled and sliced
2 tablespoons powdered or 2 whole *limou-omani*, or ¼ cup *goureh* (sour grapes) or juice of 2 lemons

آن غذائی که مرا چون جان است   غوره و جوجه و بادمجان است

That food which I most cherish is the greengrape chicken and eggplant dish.

1. In a Dutch oven, brown meat, including bone, or chicken and onions and garlic in 3 tablespoons oil. Add nutmeg, cinnamon, turmeric, salt and pepper.

2. Pour in 3 cups water with meat or 2 cups water with chicken, bring to a boil and cover. Reduce heat and simmer over low heat for about 1 hour for meat and 45 minutes for chicken.

3. Peel eggplants, cut lengthwise in quarters. Sprinkle both sides with salt and let stand for about 20 minutes. Rinse and pat dry.

4. Saute the eggplants in a skillet in the rest of the oil and set aside.

5. Add tomato paste and *limou-omani*, *goureh* or lemon juice to the meat or chicken, mix well and taste. Adjust seasoning to your taste.

6. Preheat the oven to 350°F. Pour the chicken or meat and sauce into a deep ovenproof casserole dish and arrange the eggplant and tomato slices on top. Cover and bake for 45 minutes.

7. Either serve immediately from the same dish or keep warm in oven until ready to serve.

8. Serve hot with *chelo* (page 95).

Variations: 1. Yellow split peas (¼ cup) may be added in step 5. 2. Summer squash may be substituted for eggplant.

Note: Limou-omani *(dried Persian limes)* and goureh *(sour grapes)* are available at Middle Eastern food stores (page 240).

Eggplant Stew with Chicken and Unripe Grapes, served with Chelo
Khoresh-e Goureh-o Joujeh-o Bademjan
page 152

Tea with Samovar
Chai-o Samovar
page 231

Winter Festival Setting
Corsy-e Shab-e Yalda
page 213

Potato Stew with Rice
Chelo Khoresh-e Gheimeh
page 153

Potato Stew

Makes 6 servings
Preparation time: 20 min.
Cooking time: 1 hr. 30 min.

2 onions, finely sliced
3 tablespoons oil
1 pound stewing meat, veal, lamb or beef, cut in 1-inch cubes
1 teaspoon salt
¼ teaspoon freshly ground black pepper
½ teaspoon *advieh* (allspice, page 160)
1 teaspoon cinnamon
¼ teaspoon turmeric
⅓ cup yellow split peas
3 tablespoons tomato paste
2 whole *limou-omani*, pierced, or juice of 2 lemons
¼ teaspoon saffron dissolved in 1 tablespoon hot water
1 pound or 2 large potatoes
1 cup oil for deep fry

Khoresh-e Gheimeh

1. In a Dutch oven, brown onions in 3 tablespoons oil. Add pieces of meat and saute. Add salt, pepper, *advieh*, cinnamon and turmeric. Pour in 3½ cups of water. Cover and simmer for about 1 hour over low heat, stirring occasionally.

2. Add split peas, tomato paste, *limou-omani* or lemon juice and the saffron. Cover and cook for 30 minutes more over low heat.

3. During this time, peel the potatoes and cut into strips for french fries. Wash, drain and pat dry. Fry in remaining oil.

4. Check to see that meat is done; taste sauce and correct seasoning. Pour the *khoreshe* onto a serving platter and arrange the french fries on top. Serve hot with *chelo* rice (page 95). Serve *torshi* (Persian pickles, page 164) and *sabzi-khordan* (fresh vegetables and herbs, page 8) on the side.

Note: *Limou-omani* (dried Persian limes) and *advieh* are available at food specialty shops (page 240).

Spiced Stew

Makes 6 servings
Preparation time: 20 min.
Cooking time: 1 hr.

1 fryer chicken, about 3 pounds
¼ cup oil or butter
2 onions, finely chopped
2 cloves garlic, crushed
2 large green peppers, diced
½ cup chopped fresh coriander leaves
¼ cup chopped fresh mint leaves or 2 tablespoons dried mint
1 teaspoon salt
½ teaspoon freshly ground black pepper

1 teaspoon ground cumin
1 teaspoon ground cinnamon
1 teaspoon ground coriander
½ teaspoon turmeric
1 teaspoon ground cardamom
1 teaspoon ground cloves
4 large tomatoes, peeled and sliced
2 tablespoons chick-pea flour dissolved in ½ cup water
2 tablespoons lemon juice

Khoresh-e Advieh

1. Cut the chicken into 6 pieces. Remove the fat and skins. Rinse and drain.

2. Heat the oil or butter in a Dutch oven and brown the onions and garlic. Brown the chicken. Add the green peppers, fresh coriander and mint; saute until wilted. Add the salt, pepper, spices, tomatoes and 1½ cups water. Cover and simmer over low heat for about 45 minutes, stirring occasionally.

3. Add ¼ cup cold water, dissolved chick-pea flour and lemon juice. Cover and simmer 15 minutes more.

4. Check to see if chicken is done. Taste sauce and adjust seasoning.

5. Transfer the stew to a deep casserole dish, cover and place in warm oven until ready to serve. Serve hot from the same dish with *chelo* (page 95).

Variation: Two cups yogurt mixed with ½ teaspoon ground saffron may be substituted for the tomatoes and chick-pea flour.

Yogurt Stew

Makes 6 servings
Preparation time: 15 min.
Cooking time: 1 hr.

1 fryer chicken, about 4 pounds
2 onions, finely chopped
¼ cup chopped celery (2 stalks)
2 teaspoons salt
¼ teaspoon freshly ground black
  pepper
2 cups yogurt
1 heaping tablespoon curry
  powder
1 tablespoon flour

GARNISH
⅓ cup slivered almonds
¼ cup raisins

Khoresh-e Mast

1. Cut chicken into small pieces. Remove the skin, rinse and drain.

2. In a Dutch oven, place onions, chicken and celery. Season with salt and pepper. Cover and cook for about 55 minutes over low heat.

3. In a bowl, combine yogurt with flour curry powder. Beat well with a fork.

4. When the chicken is done, stir in this mixture and simmer for 5 minutes over low heat, stirring gently and occasionally.

5. Check to be sure chicken is cooked and taste the sauce. Adjust seasoning if necessary. Transfer to a deep ovenproof casserole dish. Cover and place in warm oven until ready to serve.

6. Garnish with almonds and raisins and serve hot from same dish with *chelo* (page 95).

Variation: Curry powder and celery may be replaced with ½ teaspoon saffron and ½ cup thin sliced orange peel in syrup (page 160).

Fish Stew with Green Herbs

Makes 6 servings
Preparation time: 1 hr.
Cooking time: 1 hr.

⅓ cup kidney beans
¼ cup melted butter
2 garlic cloves, crushed
2 tablespoons chopped parsley
2 tablespoons chopped leek
½ cup chopped spinach
¼ cup chopped celery
1 tablespoon chopped fenugreek leaves
1 teaspoon salt
¼ teaspoon freshly ground black pepper
½ tablespoon turmeric
2 *limou-omani* (pierced) or juice of 2 lemons
½ cup fish stock or water
1 pound fish fillets (flounder or other white fish)

Khoresh-e Gormeh Sabzi Ba Mahi

1. In a saucepan, cook kidney beans in ½ cup water for approximately 30 minutes over medium heat.

2. Heat the butter in a skillet and saute the garlic, parsley, leek, spinach, celery and fenugreek. Combine with all the remaining ingredients in a Dutch Oven, placing the fish fillets on top. Cover and simmer over low heat for 30 minutes.

3. Transfer to deep ovenproof casserole dish. Cover and place in warm oven until ready to serve.

4. Serve hot from same dish with bread and *chelo* (page 95).

Note: *Limou-omani* (dried Persian limes) are available at Middle Eastern food shops (page 240).

PICKLES AND RELISHES

R a w   M a t e r i a l

Everyone in the teahouse was criticizing Vali. He was generally admitted to be useless; and each person had something to say against him.

"That man," said the tailor, whose words were usually considered, "is a cabbage."

Everyone murmured his assent–except Mulla.

"Not so, Aga," he said. "You must be fair. A cabbage can be boiled and eaten. What could Vali be turned into?"

Pickles   and   Relishes

Wherever the *sofreh* or cloth is spread for a meal, you will find a variety of pickles and relishes (*torshi*) accompanying the main course. Most of these *torshis* consist of vegetables or fruits and spices preserved in vinegar. For this chapter, I have selected only a few of the many kinds of *torshi* made in Iran. All are simple, traditional recipes.

Good *torshis* are made with fresh ingredients and good wine vinegar. The fruits, vegetables and herbs must be thoroughly washed and dried. Not a trace of water can remain if the *torshi* is to keep well. After the jars have been sealed, they should be stored in a cool place for aging. Once they are opened, they should be kept in the refrigerator.

Iranian Allspice

Makes ⅔ cup

لَهْ دِیه

Advieh

¼ cup dried rose petals
2 tablespoons cinnamon
1 teaspoon cardamom
½ teaspoon black pepper
1 tablespoon angelica (*gol-par*)

1 teaspoon nutmeg
1 teaspoon ground cumin

Grind all the spices and mix together. Store in an airtight container to preserve freshness.

Orange Peel in Syrup

Makes 1 jar
Preparation time: 2 hrs. while meditating or watching television
Cooking time: 30 minutes

Khoshab-e Poost-e Porteghal

3 cups slivered orange peel
   (about 10 oranges)
2 cups water
1 cup sugar

خشاب پوست پرتقال

1. Wash the oranges.

2. Peel the oranges and completely scrape off all the pith from the peel with the aid of a sharp knife. Save the oranges for a fruit salad.

3. Cut the orange peel into thin slivers

4. In order to remove all bitterness from the orange peel slivers, place them in a saucepan and cover with water, bring to a boil and cook for 10 minutes over medium heat. Then drain.

5. Return orange peel slivers to the saucepan, add 2 cups of water and 1 cup of sugar. Bring to a boil and cook for 15 minutes over medium heat. Cool and pour into a sterilized jar. Seal and keep in a cool place. Use this syrup as needed.

Mango Pickle

Makes 2 half-pints
Preparation and cooking time: 35 min.
Storage time: 6 weeks before using

2 mangoes
¼ pound tamarind
1 teaspoon *advieh* (allspice, page 160)
½ teaspoon ground saffron
1 tablespoon salt
3 cups red wine vinegar or more

Torshi-e Anbeh

1. Separate mangoes from the pits and cut into small pieces. Remove pits from tamarind. Place mangoes, tamarind, *advieh*, saffron and salt in a saucepan with 2½ cups vinegar. Bring to a boil over high heat, then reduce heat and simmer for 15 minutes. Remove from heat and let cool.

2. Sterilize canning jars in boiling water. Dry thoroughly with a clean towel. Fill the jars to within ½ inch of top, then fill to the top with vinegar and seal. This pickle should be of a thick consistency.

3. Store in a cool place for at least 6 weeks before using.

Note: *Advieh* is available at food specialty shops (page 240).

Pickled Fruits

Makes about 4 pints
Preparation and cooking time: 3 hrs.
Storage time: 10 days before using

تُرشیِ مِیوه

Torshi-e Miveh

1 pound dried apricots, chopped
¼ pound fresh or dried tamarind, pitted and chopped (optional)
¼ pound fresh ginger, finely ground
½ cup sugar
1 pound dried pitted prunes, finely chopped
1 pound dried raisins, finely chopped
1 pound apples, cored and finely chopped
1 pound quinces, cored and finely chopped

1 pound persimmons, finely chopped
2 quarts wine vinegar or more
½ teaspoon ground saffron
1 teaspoon ground cinnamon
2 tablespoons nigella seeds (*siah daneh*)
½ teaspoon cardamom
½ teaspoon cayenne pepper
2 tablespoons salt

1. Soak the apricots in water for two hours and drain. If using dried tamarind, soak it in 1 cup vinegar for 1 hour, drain and discard the seeds. Cook the ginger with ½ cup sugar and 1 cup vinegar for 15 minutes over low heat and set aside. Prepare the remaining fruit.

2. Place all the fruit in a saucepan. Cover with vinegar and simmer for about 20 minutes over medium heat. Remove from heat.

3. Add the spices and salt to the fruit and mix well.

4. Sterilize canning jars in boiling water and dry well with a towel. Fill to within ½ inch of the top with the mixture, then sprinkle each jar lightly with salt and fill to the brim with vinegar. Seal.

5. Store for at least 10 days before using.

Note: Fresh and dried tamarind and nigella seeds are available in food specialty shops (page 240).

Seven-Spice Pickle

Makes 4 pints
Preparation and cooking time: 1 hr. 15 min.
Storage time: 10 days before using

4 large or 10 small eggplants
1½ quarts wine vinegar
½ cup chopped mint leaves or 2 tablespoons dried
½ cup chopped tarragon leaves or 2 tablespoons dries
1 teaspoon peppercorns
½ cup chopped basil leaves or 2 tablespoons dried
½ cup chopped parsley or 2 tablespoons dried
½ cup chopped fenugreek leaves or 2 tablespoons dried

½ cup chopped coriander leaves or 2 tablespoons dried
½ cup chopped savory or 2 tablespoons dried
3 teaspoons salt
1 teaspoon freshly ground black pepper
½ teaspoon red pepper
2 tablespoons *gol-par*
1 tablespoon *advieh* (allspice, page 160)
8 cloves garlic, crushed

Torshi-e Hafte-bijars

1. Make a lengthwise incision in each eggplant and remove the stems (do not peel the eggplants). Wash eggplants and pat dry. Place whole eggplants in a saucepan and cover with vinegar. Cook over medium heat for 45 minutes or until tender. Drain and set aside to cool.

2. During this time, wash herbs, dry thoroughly and chop finely.

3. Place eggplants on a wooden cutting board and chop into tiny pieces. In a large bowl, combine with salt, pepper, *gol-par*, *advieh* or allspice, garlic, herbs and 1 quart vinegar. Mix thoroughly with a wooden spoon. If necessary, add more vinegar.

4. Sterilize canning jars in boiling water and dry thoroughly with a clean towel. Fill nearly to the top with *torshi* mixture. Sprinkle with salt and fill to the brim with remaining vinegar. Seal the jars.

5. Store for a least 10 days in a cool place before using.

Note: *Gol-par* (powdered angelica) and *advieh* (page 160) are available in food specialty shops (page 240).

Six-Vegetable Pickle

Makes about 4 pints
Preparation and cooking time: 2 hrs. 30 min.
Storage time: 10 days before using

Torshi-e Makhlut

2 large eggplants
2 green peppers
1 pound carrots
½ pound turnips
½ head cauliflower
2–3 celery stalks
1 pound small white onions (pearl onions)
5 cloves garlic, chopped
½ cup chopped mint leaves
½ cup chopped parsley
½ cup chopped coriander leaves
½ cup chopped basil leaves
3–4 quarts wine vinegar
2 tablespoons salt
½ teaspoon freshly ground black pepper
2 tablespoons *gol-par*
1 teaspoon *advieh* (allspice, page 160)
3 teaspoons *siah daneh*
¼ teaspoon cayenne pepper

1. Prick the eggplants with a fork to prevent bursting and bake on oven rack for 1 hour at 350°F.

2. Wash green peppers and cut into small pieces. Scrape carrots, wash and chop fine. Wash turnips and chop. Wash cauliflower and separate into small flowerets. Wash and chop celery. Clean and wash pearl onions. Peel and chop garlic cloves.

3. Wash the herbs and drain. Dry thoroughly, then chop.

4. Place baked eggplant on wooden cutting board. Remove and discard skin; chop flesh into small pieces. Sprinkle with salt. Cover with a clean towel and let stand for about 1 hour.

5. Cook chopped eggplants in 2 cups vinegar over medium heat for 10 minutes.

6. Place eggplants, 2 quarts vinegar, salt, pepper, *gol-par*, *advieh* or allspice, *siah daneh*, cayenne pepper, chopped herbs, garlic and vegetables in a large bowl. Mix well. Add more vinegar if necessary.

7. Sterilize jars in boiling water. Dry thoroughly with a clean towel. Fill to within ½ inch of the top with the mixture. Sprinkle with salt and fill to the brim with vinegar. Seal the jars.

8. Store in a cool place for at least 10 days before using.

Note: *Gol-par* (powdered angelica), *siah daneh* (nigella seeds) and *advieh* (page 160) are available in food specialty shops (page 240) catering to a Middle Eastern clientele.

Onion Pickle

Makes 4 pints
Preparation time: 30 min.
Storage time: 10 days before using

2 **pounds pearl onions, peeled**
¼ **pound garlic, crushed**
3 **sprigs of fresh tarragon**
2 **tablespoons salt**
1 **quart wine vinegar**

Torshi-e Piaz

1. Peel the onions and remove roots at the bottom. With the point of a knife, cut a cross mark in the bottom of each onion so it will absorb vinegar. Leave onion tops intact.

2. Dry onions thoroughly by spreading them on a clean towel for 5–6 hours.

3. Sterilize canning jars in boiling water and dry thoroughly.

4. Fill jars almost to the top by layering onions and garlic and sprigs of fresh herbs. Sprinkle with salt and fill to the brim with vinegar. Seal the jars and keep in a cool place.

5. Store for at least 10 days in a cool place before using. Serve as a relish with meats.

Pickled Garlic

Makes 2 pints
Preparation time: 20 min.
Storage time: 6 weeks before using

1 **pound garlic cloves**
3 **beets, washed, dried and chopped into bite-size pieces**
1 **quart vinegar**
2 **tablespoons salt**

Torshi-e Sir

1. Peel off just one outside layer of garlic cloves.

2. Sterilize large canning jars in boiling water and dry thoroughly.

3. Fill jars nearly to top with alternate layers of garlic and beets.

4. Sprinkle jars with salt and fill to the brim with vinegar. Seal the jars and keep in a cool place.

5. Store for at least 6 weeks before using.

Vegetables in Brine

Makes 6 pints
Preparation time: 40 min.
Storage time: 6 weeks before using

4 carrots
½ head of cauliflower, small
1 stalk celery
4 turnips
2 red peppers
2 pounds small pickling cucumbers
10 pearl onions
5 cloves garlic, peeled

3 sprigs of fresh dill weed
3 sprigs of fresh tarragon
3 corriander leaves
3 bay leaves
3 fresh celery leaves
3 tablespoons salt for every 2 cups water

Torshi-e Makhlut-e Shur

1. Peel carrots and clean the cauliflower, celery, turnips and red peppers. Cut into small (½-inch) pieces. Leave cucumbers, onions and garlic whole.

2. Wash and drain the vegetables. Clean, wash and drain the herbs.

3. In a large bowl, combine all the vegetables.

4. Fill each jar almost to the top in alternate layers of dill weed, tarragon, corriander, bay and celery leaves and the vegetables.

5. Boil water and salt. Fill each jar to the brim with this liquid and seal jars immediately.

6. Store for at least 6 weeks in a cool place before using.

قومی متفکرند در مذهب و دین   جمعی متحیرند در شک و یقین

ناگاه برآورد منادی ز کمین   کای بی خبران راه نه آنست و نه این

خیّام

One group are in thought of religion and the devout
Another in a quandry of certainty and doubt
Suddenly upped a messenger from his hideout
You fools! The way is neither this nor that about.

Khayyam

P R E S E R V E S

C o o k i n g   b y   C a n d l e

Mulla Nasrudin made a wager that he could spend a night on a nearby mountain and survive, in spite of ice and snow. Several wags in the teahouse agreed to adjudicate. Mulla took a book and a candle and sat through the coldest night he had ever known. In the morning, half-dead, he claimed his money.

"Did you have nothing at all to keep you warm?" asked the villagers.

"Nothing."

"Not even a candle?"

"Yes, I had a candle."

"Then you lost."

Nasrudin did not argue.

Some months later he invited the same people to a feast at his house. They sat down in his reception room, waiting for the food. Hours passed. They started to mutter about food.

"Let's go and see how it is getting on," said Mulla.

Everyone trooped into the kitchen. They found an enormous pot of water, under which a candle was burning. The water was not even tepid.

"It is not ready yet," said Mulla. "I can't understand why–it has been there since yesterday."

P r e s e r v e s

Persian preserve recipes are special because they combine fruit, flower and spice to a perfect sweetness. Besides being eaten with bread and butter, which is most often the case, these preserves are good to sweeten tea or to eat on their own as dessert.

Greengage Plum Preserves

2 pounds greengage plums
2 pounds sugar
4 cups water
¼ teaspoon citric acid
1 teaspoon ground cardamom or
  ¼ cup rosewater

Makes 4 half-pint jars
Preparation time: 40 min.
Cooking time: 35 min.

Moraba-ye Alou Zard

1. Remove stems from plums, wash and peel. (To peel plums more quickly, blanch them first for 2 minutes in boiling water; the skin will come off easily.)

2. Place sugar and water in a large saucepan. Bring to a boil, reduce heat and let simmer for 10 minutes over low heat.

3. Add the peeled plums and citric acid. Uncover and simmer for 20 minutes over low heat, stirring gently from time to time. Remove from heat, add cardamom or rosewater and allow to cool.

4. Sterilize jelly jars in boiling water. Dry thoroughly with a clean towel and fill with jam. Seal tightly.

Sour-Cherry Preserves

2 pounds pitted sour cherries
   (pitted weight)
4 cups sugar

Makes 4 half-pint jars
Preparation time: 1 hr. plus
overnight macerating
Cooking time: 50 min.

Moraba-ye Albalou

1. Wash cherries and remove stems and pits. Place cherries and sugar in large pot and macerate them overnight.

2. Bring to a boil over high heat. Reduce heat and simmer for about 35 minutes over low heat, gently stirring occasionally until the syrup has thickened. Remove foam as it forms with a skimmer. Remove from heat and let cool. If the syrup is still too thin at the end of the cooking time, remove the cherries and simmer the syrup for a few minutes longer.

3. Sterilize jelly jars in boiling water and dry thoroughly with a clean towel. Fill with preserves and seal.

Quince Preserves

Makes 4 half-pint jars
Preparation time: 25 min.
Cooking time: 2 hrs. 15 min.

2 pounds quince
1½ cups water
4 cups sugar
¼ teaspoon vanilla extract or ½ teaspoon cardamom seeds or 1 cinnamon stick
2 tablespoons lemon juice

Moraba-ye Beh

1. Cut the quinces in quarters and remove cores. Slice into ¼-inch strips. Wash and drain.

2. Place quince strips and water in a heavy saucepan. Bring to a boil over high heat, then reduce heat and let simmer over low heat for about 15 minutes. Add the sugar and the vanilla extract or cardamom seeds or cinnamon stick. Place a clean dishtowel or paper towel over pan and cover firmly with lid; this way the color will turn red. Let simmer over low heat for 1 hour.

3. Add lemon juice. Cover and simmer for 1 hour more over low heat, stirring gently from time to time, until the syrup has thickened and the quince has turned red. Remove from heat and allow to cool.

4. Sterilize jelly jars in boiling water and dry. Fill with preserves. Seal jars.

Fig Preserves

Makes 4 half-pint jars
Preparation time: 5 min. plus
overnight macerating
Cooking time: 1 hr.

2 **pounds firm seedless green figs**
3½ **cups sugar**
½ **teaspoon citric acid**
2½ **cups water**
½ **teaspoon vanilla extract or ¼ cup rosewater**

Moraba-ye Anjir

1. Wash figs and pierce them once with a toothpick. Place in heavy pot and add sugar. Macerate overnight.

2. The next day, add citric acid and water. Cover, bring to a boil over low heat, then uncover and simmer for about 1 hour or until the syrup has thickened enough to coat the back of a spoon. Remove from heat, add vanilla extract or rosewater and allow to cool.

3. Sterilize jelly jars in boiling water and dry thoroughly. Fill with preserves and seal.

Carrot Preserves

Makes 4 half-pint jars
Preparation time: 15 min.
Cooking time: 1 hr. 10 min.

2 **pounds carrots**
1 **cup slivered orange peel**
8 **cups sugar**
2 **cups water**
⅓ **cup lemon juice**
½ **teaspoon ground cardamom**

Moraba-ye Havij

1. Scrape and shred carrots; wash and drain.

2. Put the slivered orange peel in a saucepan with water. Boil for 10 minutes.

3. Combine sugar, water, lemon juice, orange peel and carrots in a heavy saucepan. Bring to a boil over high heat, then reduce heat and simmer for 1 hour or until syrup has thickened. Remove from heat, stir in cardamom and allow to cool.

4. Sterilize jelly jars in boiling water and dry thoroughly. Fill with preserves and seal.

Rose Petal Jelly

1 pound fresh rose petals
½ cup lime or lemon juice
2½ cups water
2 cups sugar

Makes 2 half-pint jars
Preparation time: 20 min.
Cooking time: 1 hr.

Moraba-ye Gol-e Sorkh

1. Select fresh pink and red rose petals. Make sure they have not been sprayed with insecticide. Cut off the white ends, wash carefully, drain and place in a bowl. Sprinkle with half the lime or lemon juice and marinate for 10 minutes.

2. Place the rose petals and water in a heavy saucepan. Bring to a boil over high heat, reduce heat and simmer for 20 to 45 minutes or until the petals are tender.

3. Add sugar and the rest of the lime juice. Simmer 15 minutes longer, stirring constantly, until the syrup has thickened. Remove from heat and allow to cool.

4. Sterilize jelly jars in boiling water. Dry thoroughly. Fill with jelly and seal.

Note: Dried rose petals may be used in place of fresh rose petals. Rose petals are available at food specialty shops (page 240).

Orange Blossom Jelly

½ **pound fresh orange blossoms**
½ **pound sugar**
½ **cup water**
2 **teaspoons lemon juice**

Makes 1 half-pint jar
Preparation time: 35 min. plus 1
day's marination
Cooking time: 25 min.

Moraba-ye Bahar Narenj

1. Carefully wash the orange blossoms and soak in a bowl of cold water. Set in refrigerator for a day, changing the water several times.

2. Bring the blossoms and 1 cup water to a boil in a heavy saucepan, over high heat. Pour out the water, drain the blossoms and repeat. This step is essential to remove traces of bitterness.

3. In a heavy saucepan, bring the sugar and water to a boil, then reduce heat and add orange blossoms. Simmer for 15 minutes. Add lemon juice and simmer 15 minutes longer until the syrup has thickened enough to coat the back of a spoon. Remove from heat and allow to cool.

4. Sterilize jelly jars in boiling water. Dry thoroughly with a clean towel. Fill with jelly and seal.

Plum Paste Rolls

6 **pounds ripe greengage plums**
⅓ **cup water**
½ **teaspoon salt**

Preparation time: 30 min.
Cooking time: 45 min.

Lavashak

Lavashak is a special treat that many Iranian children prefer to chocolate. It is a kind of fruit paste and it can be prepared with many different fruits, such as apricots, berries, cherries and any kind of plum. It is particularly good when made with greengage plums.

1. Wash plums and place in a large pot with water and salt. Cook over medium heat, stirring constantly to prevent sticking to the bottom, for 30 to 45 minutes or until the flesh falls away from the pit.

2. Transfer fruit to a colander placed over a bowl. Press out all the juice and flesh, until only the pits and skin are left. The pulp should be of a creamy consistency. Or prepare the pulp in a food processor, removing the peels and pits first.

3. Pour a layer ¼ inch thick into several round or oval dishes. Set out to dry in direct sunlight for 4 to 5 days.

4. Detach the edges of the paste with the point of a knife. Peel off and wrap in clear plastic wrap.

PASTRIES AND BREADS

شعراست هیچ و شاعری این هیچ هم تر   در حیرتم که در هنر سی این جدا ا ست

شعر اصلش از خیال جنبش ازل   تا از خیال این همه فکر محال ست

سحاب

The poem is nothing and the poet less than nothing
I am amazed by all this contention over nothing
The poem's source is the imagination its substance the
*   impossible*
'Till when and why from the imagination all this
*   thought of the impossible.*

Sahab

Pastries   and   Breads

Iranian pastries were refined during the foodie Qajar era of the 19th Century. Although these pastries are very delicate, the recipes that follow are simple and well worth trying. As for the bread, perhaps only the *parisienne baguette* can compete with *nan-e barbari*.

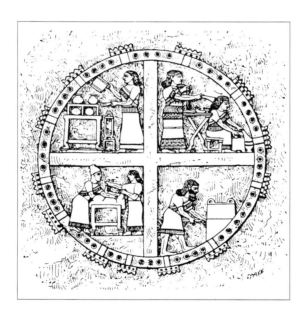

Rice Cookies

Makes 36 pieces
Preparation time: 30 min. plus 6
hrs. resting time
Cooking time: 20 min.

2¼ cups rice flour
5 egg yolks
1½ cups confectioners sugar
¼ cup rosewater
1 cup unsalted melted butter
1 tablespoon cardamom
Poppy seeds for garnish

Nan-e Berenji

1. Spread rice flour in a large tray and place in a warm oven for several hours. This way it will dry thoroughly.

2. In a bowl, beat the egg yolks with the sugar, rosewater and melted butter until creamy.

3. Add rice flour and cardamom to the egg mixture gradually, stirring constantly. Knead well to produce a dough that does not stick to the hands. Cover the bowl with a clean damp towel and set aside to rest for 6 hours at room temperature.

4. Spread a sheet of wax paper on a cookie sheet. Take a spoonful of dough, roll it into a ball the size of a hazelnut, flatten slightly and place on wax paper. Leave 2½ inches between balls. With a fork, draw geometric patterns on the cookies and garnish with poppy seeds.

5. Place cookie sheet in the center of the oven, heat to 325° and bake for 15 to 20 minutes. *Nan-e berenji* must remain white.

6. Remove from oven. Cool. These cookies crumble very easily; remove them carefully from wax paper.

7. Arrange in a pyramid on a footed cake dish.

Note: Rice flour (ground rice) is available at food specialty shops (page 240) and health food stores.

Rice Cookies
Nan-e Berenji
page 184

White Mulberries
Toote
page 197

Saffron Cake
Halva
page 210

Saffron Pudding
Sholeh Zard
page 206

Chick-pea Cookies
Nan-e Nokhodchi
page 185

Baklava
Baghlava
page 186

Chick-pea Cookies

Makes 36 pieces
Preparation time: 30 min. plus ½ hr. rising time
Cooking time: 30 min.

1 cup unsalted butter
1 egg yolk
2 cups roasted chick-pea flour, sifted
1 teaspoon ground cardamom
1 cup confectioners sugar
1 tablespoon slivered pistachio nuts

Nan-e Nokhodchi

1. Melt the butter and beat until it becomes white. Add egg yolk and beat until creamy. Blend in flour, cardamom and sugar, stirring constantly to produce a dough. Knead well with your hands until the dough no longer sticks to your hands.

2. Cover and let stand for ½ hour.

3. Roll the dough out to a ¼ inch thickness and cut out cookies with a tiny cloverleaf cookie cutter. Decorate each cookie with slivered pistachio nuts. Cover a cookie sheet with wax paper and place each cookie on the sheet, leaving 2 inches between pieces to allow them to spread.

4. Place the cookie sheet in the center of the oven. Heat to 300°F and bake for 20 to 30 minutes, until slightly golden. Remove from oven, cool and carefully lift cookies off wax paper.

5. Arrange in a pyramid on a platter.

Note: Chick-pea flour is available in food specialty shops (page 240), health food stores and sometimes on the gourmet shelf of the supermarket.

Baklava

Makes 12 pieces
Preparation time: 50 min.
Cooking time: 40 min.

Baghlava

FILLING
¾ cup blanched almonds, ground
¾ cup shelled pistachio nuts, ground
½ cup granulated sugar
1 teaspoon ground cardamom
¼ pound unsalted butter, melted
1 package (1 pound) frozen filo pastry dough
2 tablespoons ground pistachio nuts for garnish

SYRUP
1½ cups sugar
1 cup water
½ cup rosewater

1. In a food processor, finely grind the almonds and pistachios together.

2. In a bowl, combine the sugar, cardamom powder and the almond and pistachio mixture. Mix well.

3. Preheat oven to 350°F. Grease a 13-inch baking pan. Cut the dough with scissors so it will be the same size as the baking pan. When working with this dough, do not unwrap all of it at the same time, since it dries out very quickly.

4. Place 1 layer of dough on the bottom of the pan. Using a pastry brush, paint it with melted butter. Repeat for 2 more layers, painting each layer of dough with melted butter.

5. Evenly sprinkle 3 tablespoons of the almond, pistachio and cardamom mixture on top of this. Continue building up with layers of dough brushed with melted butter and sprinkled with the walnut mixture, ending with 3 layers of dough on top.

6. Place the pan with the pastry in preheated oven and bake 20 to 25 minutes or until the baklava is golden brown.

7. For the syrup, place sugar and water in a saucepan. Boil over medium heat for 15 minutes. Add the rosewater and set aside.

8. Remove from oven. Pour rosewater syrup over the baklava and decorate with ground pistachio nuts.

9. Using a spatula, lift the pieces out of the baking pan and carefully arrange pieces of pastry one by one on a cake dish.

Variations: 1. Honey (½ cup) may be substituted for the syrup. 2. To make the dough from scratch, follow these directions: Combine ½ cup milk, ½ teaspoon baking powder, 3 tablespoons melted butter and 3 egg yolks in a mixing bowl. Slowly blend in 1 cup flour, stirring constantly to form a dough which does not stick to the hands. Knead well. Cover with a clean towel and let rise for 3 hours. Place a piece of dough the size of a walnut on a floured pastry board and roll out very thin with a rolling pin. Use in the same manner as frozen filo dough, but use 1 layer of dough for the bottom and 1 layer of dough for the top.

This sweet flaky pastry, filled with chopped nuts and topped with sugar syrup, has come to be known—and enjoyed!—worldwide. The Persian version uses a combination of chopped almonds and pistachios spiced with cardamom and a rosewater-scented syrup. It is a subtle, delicate blend of flavors. While many Persians still make the thin dough at home, frozen filo pastry, which is ready to use, is an acceptable alternative.

Walnut Cookies

Makes 30 pieces
Preparation time: 30 min.
Cooking time: 45 min.

3 egg yolks
½ cup sugar
1½ cups coarsely chopped walnuts
2 tablespoons ground pistachio nuts

نان گردوئی

Nan-e Gerdoui

1. In a bowl, combine egg yolks and sugar and beat thoroughly. Add chopped walnuts and mix with a wooden spoon.

2. Spread a piece of wax paper on a cookie sheet. Drop batter by the teaspoonful on the wax paper, leaving about 2½ inches between cookies. Decorate each one with a small amount of ground pistachio nuts.

3. Bake 35 to 45 minutes in a 300°F oven (do not preheat oven). Remove from oven and cool. Lift cookies off wax paper.

4. Arrange on a serving dish.

Almond Cookies

Makes 20 pieces
Preparation time: 40 min.
Cooking time: 20 min.

Nan-e Badami

3 egg yolks
1 cup sugar
1½ cups ground almonds
4 teaspoons cardamom powder
1 teaspoon baking soda
1 tablespoon rosewater

1. In a large bowl, beat egg yolks until creamy. Slowly mix in the sugar, ground almonds, cardamom, baking soda and rosewater. Knead well with your hands.

2. Preheat oven to 250°F. Place a sheet of wax paper on a cookie sheet.

3. Scoop out some of the batter with a teaspoon and roll it into a small ball the size of a hazelnut. Flatten the piece of dough with your hand and place it on the wax paper. Continue, leaving about 2½ inches room between balls for them to rise.

4. Place cookie sheet in preheated oven and bake for 20 minutes, until golden.

5. Remove from oven, allow to cool and remove cookies from wax paper. Keep in cookie jar.

6. When ready to serve, arrange in a pyramid on a footed cake dish.

Variation: This cookie may be made using egg whites in place of egg yolks. The result is completely different.

Coconut Cookies

Makes 40 pieces
Preparation time: 25 min.
Cooking time: 20 min.

¾ cup unsalted butter
2½ cups confectioners sugar
2 cups flour
1 teaspoon ground cardamom
2 cups shredded unsweetened coconut

Nan-e Nargili

1. In a bowl, combine butter and confectioners sugar and beat well until creamy. Blend in the flour and cardamom. Add coconut, stirring constantly to make a dough. Knead it well to produce a dough that does not stick to your hands.

2. Spread a piece of wax paper on a cookie sheet.

3. On a pastry board, roll the dough out ½ inch thick with a rolling pin. Cut it into pieces shaped to your desire using a floured cookie cutter.

4. Place pieces on the wax paper, leaving 2½ inches between them to allow them to expand. Bake in 300°F oven for about 20 minutes until golden.

5. Remove from oven. Allow to cool and remove from wax paper.

6. Arrange in a pyramid on a footed cake dish or platter.

Elephant Ears

Makes 25 pieces
Preparation time: 45 min. plus 3
hrs. for dough to rise
Cooking time: 30 min.

2 egg yolks
2 tablespoons oil
¼ cup rosewater
2 cups flour
3 cups corn or peanut oil for frying

GARNISH
1 cup confectioners sugar
1 teaspoon ground cardamom
2 tablespoons ground pistachio nuts

Goush-e Fil

1. In a bowl, beat the egg yolks and oil until creamy. Add rosewater and slowly blend in flour, stirring constantly. Knead well to produce a dough that does not stick to the hands. Cover the bowl with a clean towel or wrap dough in plastic wrap and set aside for 3 hours at room temperature.

2. Mix confectioners sugar with cardamom and set aside.

3. Using a rolling pin, roll out the dough on a pastry board until paper thin. Cut the rolled dough into circles 3 inches in diameter, using a cookie cutter. Gather each circle across the middle—like a bow—and pinch to make it hold its shape.

4. Heat the oil in a deep pan or deep-fat fryer over medium heat to 375°F. Drop the bows into the hot oil and fry until golden on both sides (about 30 seconds).

5. Drain in a colander. Sprinkle with the mixture of powdered sugar and ground cardamom. Garnish with ground pistachio nuts.

6. Arrange on a serving platter.

Variation: Filo dough may be used instead of making dough from scratch.

Almond Rolls

Makes 20 pieces
Preparation time: 1 hr. plus 3 hrs.
for dough to rise
Cooking time: 30 min.

DOUGH
- 2 egg yolks
- ½ cup unsalted butter
- ½ cup plain yogurt
- ½ teaspoon baking powder
- 1½ cups flour

FILLING
- ¼ cup confectioners sugar
- 1 cup ground almonds or walnuts
- ½ teaspoon ground cardamom

- 3 cups oil for frying
- ½ cup powdered sugar for dusting or dipping

Ghottab

1. For the dough, combine egg yolks, butter, yogurt and baking powder in a bowl. Slowly blend in flour, stirring constantly. Knead well with hands to produce a dough which does not stick to the hands. Cover the bowl with a clean towel or place the dough in a plastic bag and set aside to rise for 3 hours at room temperature.

2. Meanwhile, prepare filling by mixing together sugar, almonds and cardamom in a bowl.

3. On a floured pastry board, roll the dough out ⅙ inch thick and 3 inches in diameter with a rolling pin. Cut the dough into small circles, using a glass dipped in flour or a floured cookie cutter.

4. Place 2 teaspoons of filling in the center of each circle of dough. Wet the edges with cold water and fold one half over the other to form a half-moon. Using a fork, press the dough around the filling to seal it.

5. Heat the oil in a deep saucepan or deep-fat fryer to 375°F and carefully slip the *ghottab* one by one into the hot oil. Do not crowd. Fry on low heat until golden brown on both sides (about 5–9 minutes). Drain in a colander or on paper towels. Sprinkle with powdered sugar.

6. Arrange in a pyramid on a serving platter.

Lady's Fingers

Makes 15 pieces
Preparation time: 30 min.
Cooking time: 25 min.

ROSEWATER SYRUP
1 cup water
2½ cups sugar
½ cup lemon juice
2 tablespoons rosewater

DOUGH
½ cup water
¼ teaspoon saffron, dissolved in 3 tablespoons hot water
5 tablespoons butter
1 cup flour
3 eggs, beaten

3 cups oil for frying

Bamieh

Bamieh *and* zoulbia *(sweet fritters, page 194) are served as dessert after dinner or with tea to sweeten it instead of sugar.*

1. For the syrup, bring the water to a boil in a saucepan. Add sugar and boil for 5 minutes. Add lemon juice and rosewater. Boil 5 minutes longer. Set aside.

2. For the dough, bring ½ cup water to boil in a saucepan. Add the saffron and butter and stir. Boil for 5 minutes. Gradually add the flour, stirring constantly with a fork to produce a smooth, elastic dough. Remove from heat and allow to cool. Add the eggs one at a time and mix thoroughly.

3. Fill several pastry bags or a clean plastic squeeze bottle (like a ketchup dispenser) with dough. Heat oil in a deep saucepan or deep-fat fryer to 375°F.

4. Squeeze small finger-size pieces of dough from the pastry bag or bottle directly into the hot oil. Fry until golden on all sides.

5. Using a skimmer or slotted spoon, gently remove the *bamieh* from the oil. Drain in a colander and let cool. Dip in rosewater syrup, making sure each piece is thoroughly soaked on all sides, and arrange on a serving platter.

Sweet Fritters

Makes 20 pieces
Preparation time: 1 hr.
Cooking time: 20 min.

زولبـیا

Zoulbia

These pretzel-shaped fritters can be made with either a yeast or a baking powder dough. Either way, the result is a sweet and light fluffy fritter. Zoulbia is often part of the fast-breaking ceremony during the month of Ramadan.

SYRUP
1 cup water
2 cups sugar
¼ cup rosewater
Juice of 1 lemon
3 tablespoons honey

BAKING POWDER DOUGH
1½ teaspoons baking powder
1 cup lukewarm water
1½ cups all-purpose flour
2 teaspoons lemon juice
3 cups corn or peanut oil for frying

1. To make the syrup, place water, sugar, rosewater, lemon juice and honey in a saucepan. Bring to a boil over high heat. Reduce heat and simmer 10 minutes over low heat. Set aside.

2. To prepare dough, dissolve baking powder in 1 cup water in a bowl. Add flour and lemon juice. Mix thoroughly until creamy and set aside for 30 to 45 minutes.

3. Fill several clean plastic squeeze bottles (like a ketchup dispenser) with dough. Heat oil in a deep-fat fryer to 375°F.

4. Hold bottle over fryer and squeeze dough in a pretzel shape directly into oil. Fry until golden brown on all sides.

5. With a skimmer or slotted spoon, gently remove *zoulbia* from oil. Dip in syrup, covering all sides.

6. Using another, clean skimmer, remove the pieces and arrange on a serving platter. (It is helpful to have two persons for cooking at this point; one person to place the dough in the oil and one person to remove them.)

Note: A yeast dough may be used to make sweet fritters. Mix 1½ cups all-purpose flour with 1 cup lukewarm water and 1 scant tablespoon of dry yeast. Beat with an electric mixer until creamy and set aside for 20 minutes. Follow the main recipe for cooking the dough and preparing the syrup.

Window Cookies

Makes 30 cookies
Preparation time: 10 min.
Cooking time: 30 min.

1 cup cornstarch
1 cup milk
1 tablespoon rosewater
5 egg yolks
2 tablespoons flour
4 cups frying oil

GARNISH
1 cup confectioners sugar
1 teaspoon ground cardamom

Nan-e Panjarehi

1. Combine confectioners sugar with cardamom. Mix well and set aside.

2. Dissolve the cornstarch in the milk. Add rosewater.

3. Beat the egg yolks until creamy; add flour and mix well. Add the cornstarch and milk mixture and beat well.

4. Heat a large pot or deep fat fryer with 4 cups of oil.

5. Heat a rosette iron (mold) by dipping it in the hot oil. Shake the iron well and let the excess oil run off. Dip immediately into the batter. It is very important that the mold is dipped in the batter to just below the top edge.

6. Plunge the coated iron into the hot oil. Shake well while it is cooking. This way the iron will separate from the cookies and lift out easily. Cook until golden. (It is helpful to have two persons for cooking at this point; one person to place the cookies in the oil and one person to remove them.)

7. Remove the iron from the oil and remove the cookie from the oil with a fork. Place a paper towel in a large tray and drain cookies. Let cool. Repeat this process until all batter is used, occasionally stirring the batter to avoid separation of cornstarch and milk.

8. When cookies are cool, sprinkle with cardamom-flavored confectioners sugar. Cookies should be golden and crispy.

Honey Almonds

Makes 25 pieces
Preparation time: 15 min.
Cooking time: 40 min.

سوهان عسلی

Sohan Assali

1 cup sugar
1 tablespoon pure honey
3 tablespoons unsalted butter
2 cups slivered almonds
½ teaspoon ground saffron, dissolved in 2 tablespoons hot water
2 tablespoons chopped pistachio nuts

1. Melt the sugar gently in a saucepan, then add the honey and butter. Cook over low heat, stirring constantly.

2. Add slivered almonds to the honey mixture. Stir from time to time, until mixture is firm and golden brown. Add the saffron and cook 5 minutes longer over low heat, stirring occasionally.

3. Place a piece of wax paper on a cookie sheet. Place wooden teaspoonfuls of the mixture on the wax paper, leaving a 1-inch space between each. Garnish with chopped pistachio nuts.

4. Allow to cool, then remove from paper.

5. Arrange on a serving platter. Cover with a sheet of aluminum foil to keep *sohan assali* crisp. Keep in an airtight container or cookie jar.

White Mulberries

Makes 25 pieces
Preparation time: 30 min.

1 cup ground almonds
1 teaspoon ground cardamom
1 cup confectioners sugar
3 tablespoons rosewater
1 tablespoon orange flower water

1 cup granulated sugar
2 tablespoons slivered pistachio nuts

Toote

1. Mix ground almonds, cardamom and confectioners sugar in a bowl. Slowly blend in rosewater and orange flower water, stirring constantly, to make a soft dough.

2. Take small spoonfuls of dough and shape into 1-inch "white mulberries." Roll each in granulated sugar and attach a sliver of pistachio as a stem.

3. Arrange on a serving platter and cover tightly with plastic wrap to keep them from drying out. Store in an airtight container or cookie jar.

Note: Orange flower water is available at food specialty shops (page 240).

Barbari Bread

Makes 11 loaves
Preparation time: 40 min. plus 6
hrs. rising time
Cooking time: 12 min.

1 package or 1 scant tablespoon dry yeast	4 tablespoons oil or butter
3 cups warm water	½ cup yellow corn meal
1 teaspoon sugar	1 tablespoon sesame seeds
1 teaspoon salt	
8½ cups all-purpose flour or more	

نان بربری

Nan-e Barbari

1. Dissolve yeast in 1 cup warm water. Add sugar and set aside for 10 minutes.

2. Pour the yeast mixture in a large bowl or in a food processer, add 2 cups warm water, salt and mix well, gradually adding the flour and stirring constantly. When 6 cups of flour have been added, knead by hand, adding the rest of the flour if necessary, until the dough is no longer sticky.

3. Pour the oil in another large bowl and place dough over it. Cover entirely with a clean damp towel and allow to rise for 4 hours in a warm, dark place (oven or pantry) without moving.

4. Punch air out of dough while it is still in the bowl; flip it over and return it to the bowl. Cover with a new damp towel and allow to rise for 2 hours more.

5. Place a cookie sheet in the center of the oven and preheat to 500°F.

6. Divide the dough into 11 parts, each piece about 5 inches in diameter. Dust a tray with the corn meal and place loaves on the tray. With damp hands, press fingertips into each loaf, then sprinkle tops with sesame seeds.

7. Put loaves on the cookie sheet, corn meal side down, and bake sesame side for 8 minutes in closed oven. Turn bread over and bake corn meal side for 4 minutes in closed oven.

8. Remove loaves from oven. Cover with a clean towel, serve it hot or wrap in aluminum foil and save in freezer. Toast before serving.

Barbari bread is a flat, 1–1½-inch thick loaf. It may be made in a round or oval shape. It is at its best eaten fresh, like French bread, but it may be frozen in aluminum foil. If frozen, toast before serving.

Lavash Bread

Makes 20 small loaves
Preparation time: 40 min. plus 5
hrs. rising time
Cooking time: 1 to 3 min.

½ package or ½ scant tablespoon
    dry yeast
1 teaspoon sugar
1 cup warm water
2½ pounds all-purpose flour
1 teaspoon salt

½ cup melted butter
2 cups milk
1 cup yogurt

Nan-e Lavash

*Made from wheat flour, Lavash is
light, crusty and the oldest known
bread in the Middle East. It comes
in various shapes—round or
oval—and is about 2 feet wide.
Since it keeps well for long periods
at a time, it is baked only once
every few months, in a tanour or
bread oven. Then it is wrapped in
clean cloths and eaten as needed.
A simplified recipe is given here.*

1. Dissolve yeast and sugar in water in a bowl. Allow to ferment for 10 minutes in a warm place.

2. In a large bowl or in a food processor, sift the flour with the salt. Gradually add the yeast mixture, the butter and the milk, stirring constantly. Add more warm water if necessary to make a firm dough. Knead on a floured surface until the dough is supple and elastic. Cover with a clean towel and allow to rise for 2 hours in a warm place.

3. Turn the dough onto a floured surface and knead for 3 minutes. Cover again and leave to rise for 1 hour.

4. Working on a floured surface, knead the dough for 15 minutes by hand. Divide it into about 20 pieces the size of an apple. Place each ball on a lightly-floured wooden board with a handle, and use a rolling pin to roll each ball out as thin as possible to a diameter of about 12 inches. Paint each loaf with yogurt.

5. Place a cookie sheet in the oven and preheat to 500°F. Flip the dough off the board onto the cookie sheet and bake for 5 to 7 minutes. Remove from oven. Wrap lavash in a clean towel and set aside for 10 minutes while the towel absorbs the moisture, then remove the towel and wrap the bread in aluminum foil, a plastic bag or a clean cloth.

6. Continue until all dough is baked.

نرمک نرمک نسیم   زیر گلان می خرد

غبغب این می مکد،   عارض آن می بَرد

گیسوی این می کشد،   گردن آن می گزد

گه به چمن می چمد،   گه به سمن می وزد

گاه به شاخ درخت،   گه به لب جویبار

Softly softly the breeze
Wafts under the flowers
Kisses the chin of one
Strokes the face of another
Pulls the hair of one
Bites the neck of another
Falls a moment to the grass
Blows a while on the jasmine
A moment on the branch
A while by the stream

Gha'ani

D E S S E R T S

گلی خوشبوی در حمام روزی رسید از دست محبوبی بدستم

بدو گفتم که مشکی یا عبیری که از بوی دلاویز تو مستم

بگفتا من گلی ناچیز بودم ولیکن مدتی با گل نشستم

کمال همنشین در من اثر کرد وگرنه من همان خاکم که هستم

سعدی

A sweet-smelling piece of clay*, one day in the bath, came from the hand of a beloved one to my hand. I asked: "Are you musk or ambergris? Because your delicious odor intoxicates me." It replied: "I was a worthless lump of clay, but for a while in the society of a rose. The perfection of my companion took effect on me, otherwise, I am the same earth which I am."

Sa'di

*balls of perfumed clay were used instead of soap.

D e s s e r t s

The rice desserts of Iran are served at any time of the day, not just at the end of a meal. Some are associated with special events.

Katchi, a saffron cream, for example, is eaten by new mothers on the first and fifth days after giving birth as part of a ceremony in which a holy person whispers the newborn child's name in his or her ear. It is also very good for nursing mothers.

Halva, a saffron cake, is prepared during the first three days after a death and after the eve of the seventh and fortieth days of mourning. It is offered to family, friends and the poor.

Sholeh zard, a saffron pudding, is reserved for the holiday in remembrance of the dead. It serves as an offering to the poor or as thanksgiving for a wish come true.

All of these dishes may be eaten hot or cold. I prefer to serve them well chilled. They may be presented in individual dishes or in a large serving bowl.

Rice Pudding

Makes 6 servings
Preparation time: 5 min.
Cooking time: 45 min.

½ cup rice
1½ cups water
5 cups milk
¼ cup rosewater
1 teaspoon ground cardamom
1 cup half and half or cream

Shir Berenj

1. Wash and drain rice. Place in a saucepan with 1½ cups water and cook, covered, over low heat for 15 minutes or until the rice is tender.

2. Add milk and cook 25 minutes longer over low heat, stirring frequently, until the mixture has thickened. Add rosewater, cardamom and half and half and cook 5 minutes more, stirring constantly.

3. Remove from heat. Arrange in a serving bowl or in individual bowls, chill in refrigerator and serve with sugar, jam or honey.

Rice Cream

½ cup rice flour (ground rice)
5 cups milk
½ cup sugar
¼ cup rosewater

Makes 6 servings
Preparation time: 5 min.
Cooking time: 30 min.

Fereni

1. Combine rice flour, milk and sugar in a saucepan and cook 25 minutes over low heat, stirring frequently, until the mixture has thickened. Add rosewater and cook 5 minutes more, stirring constantly.

2. Remove from heat. Arrange in a serving bowl or in individual bowls, chill in refrigerator and serve with sugar, jam or honey.

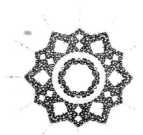

Saffron Pudding

Makes 8 servings
Preparation time: 5 min.
Cooking time: 1 hour 30 min.

شُله‌زرد

Sholeh Zard

1½ cups rice
6 cups water
3 cups sugar
⅓ cup butter, melted
1 teaspoon slivered almonds
¼ teaspoon ground saffron, dissolved in 2 tablespoons hot water
1 teaspoon ground cardamom
¼ cup rosewater

GARNISH
2 teaspoons ground cinnamon
2 teaspoons slivered almonds
2 teaspoons slivered pistachio nuts

1. Wash the rice, changing the water several times. Drain.

2. Combine rice with 6 cups water in a large saucepan and bring to a boil, skimming the foam from the surface as it forms. Simmer for 35 minutes over medium heat.

3. Add sugar and cook 15 minutes more, stirring constantly. Add the butter, almonds, dissolved saffron, cardamom and rosewater. Mix well. Cover and simmer over low heat for 40 minutes, stirring occasionally, until mixture has thickened to a pudding.

4. Spoon into individual serving dishes or a large bowl. Decorate with cinnamon, almonds and pistachio nuts. Chill in refrigerator.

5. Serve cold.

Cornstarch Pudding

Makes 6 servings
Preparation time: 5 min.
Cooking time: 30 min.

1 cup cornstarch
6 cups water
2 cups sugar
¼ cup rosewater
½ cup slivered almonds
½ cup butter, melted

1 teaspoon ground cardamom
3 tablespoons slivered almonds
for garnish

Masghati Kasehi

1. Dissolve cornstarch in 6 cups cool water in a saucepan. Bring to a boil, reduce heat and simmer about 15 minutes, stirring constantly, until mixture has thickened.

2. Add sugar, rosewater, almonds, butter and cardamom. Mix thoroughly. Simmer 15 minutes longer or until it thickens to a pudding consistency. Remove from heat.

3. Transfer to a serving dish. Garnish with slivered almonds. Chill in refrigerator.

4. Serve cold.

Paradise Custard

Makes 6 servings
Preparation time: 10 min.
Cooking time: 35 min.

Yakh Dar Behesht

1 cup rice flour (ground rice)
3 cups milk
1 cup cornstarch
1 cup water
1½ cups sugar
1 cup rosewater

GARNISH
⅓ cup slivered almonds, toasted
1 teaspoon chopped pistachio nuts

1. Dissolve the rice flour in 3 cups milk and the cornstarch in 1 cup cool water. Combine in a saucepan and mix well. Simmer over low heat, stirring constantly, until the mixture comes to a boil.

2. Add sugar and rosewater. Simmer 15 minutes longer, until the mixture reaches the consistency of a pudding, stirring constantly to prevent sticking. Remove from heat.

3. Transfer to a serving bowl. Decorate with toasted almonds and pistachio nuts.

4. Chill in refrigerator. Serve cool.

Date Cakes

Makes 15 pieces
Preparation time: 30 min.
Cooking time: 30 min.

⅓ pound coarsely chopped walnuts
1 pound pitted dates, chopped
2 teaspoons ground cinnamon
1 teaspoon ground cardamom
2 cups flour

½ cup unsalted butter
½ cup confectioners sugar
1 tablespoon chopped pistachio nuts or shredded coconut

Ranguinak

1. In a skillet, grill the walnuts over low heat for 5 minutes.

2. Add the dates to the walnuts in the skillet; mix well.

3. Combine ground cinnamon and cardamom and set aside.

4. In a large, deep skillet, saute flour in butter over medium heat, stirring constantly, until the mixture is thoroughly golden brown (caramel color).

5. Add confectioners sugar and half of the cinnamon and cardamom mixture to the flour in the skillet. Mix thoroughly over medium heat for 3 minutes, then remove from heat.

6. Arrange the dates and walnuts in a flat dish or cookie sheet and spread the dough on them. Pack and smooth well with a spoon or spatula. Sprinkle with the remaining cinnamon and cardamom mixture. Decorate with chopped pistachio nuts or shredded coconut. Refrigerate.

6. Cut into small square-shaped pieces. Carefully arrange these on a serving platter.

Saffron Cake

Makes 6 servings
Preparation time: 10 min.
Cooking time: 45 min.

1 cup unsalted butter
2 cups sifted all-purpose flour
⅓ cup water
1 cup sugar
½ teaspoon ground saffron,
  dissolved in ¼ cup hot water

¼ cup rosewater
½ teaspoon ground cardamom
2 tablespoons ground pistachio
  nuts for garnish

Halva

1. In a large, deep skillet, melt the butter and stir in the flour gradually, stirring constantly with a wooden spoon. Fry over medium heat for about 20 minutes or until it is golden brown (caramel color). Remove from heat.

2. Bring the water and sugar to a boil in a saucepan. Remove from heat and add saffron, rosewater and ground cardamom. Mix well.

3. Gradually stir this syrup into the still-hot flour and butter mixture, stirring quickly and constantly with a wooden spoon to make a thick, smooth paste.

4. Transfer to a flat plate and pack firmly with a spoon. Decorate by making geometric patterns with a spoon and garnish with ground pistachio nuts.

5. Chill in refrigerator. Cut into small pieces and serve cold as a main dish with bread or alone as a dessert.

Saffron Cream

Makes 6 servings
Preparation time: 10 min.
Cooking time: 45 min.

Katchi

1 cup butter
2 cups sifted all-purpose flour or rice flour
2 cups water
2 cups sugar
1 teaspoon ground saffron, dissolved in ¼ cup hot water
¼ cup rosewater
½ teaspoon ground cardamom

GARNISH
2 tablespoons slivered almonds
2 tablespoons slivered pistachio nuts

1. In a large, deep skillet, melt the butter and stir in the flour gradually, stirring constantly with a wooden spoon. Cook over medium heat for about 20 minutes or until it is golden brown (caramel color).

2. Bring the water and sugar to a boil in a saucepan. Add saffron, rosewater and ground cardamom and gradually stir in the flour and butter mixture, stirring quickly and constantly with a wooden spoon. Simmer until the mixture reaches a creamy consistency. You may add more water if it becomes too thick.

3. Transfer to a serving bowl. Garnish with almonds and pistachio nuts before serving.

Katchi *is a liquid form of* halva. *It is made the same way, but with three times the amount of water.* Katchi *is served hot.*

Yogurt

2 **quarts whole milk**
1 **cup plain yogurt**
1 **cup half and half**

Makes 8 servings
Preparation time: 20 min. plus 12
hrs. setting time

Mast

1. Bring milk to a boil in a very clean pot (dirty or greasy utensils will not produce the desired results).

2. Remove from heat and pour into a glass jar or pottery container; let stand until cool.

3. Dilute yogurt in 1 cup cool milk and 1 cup half and half. Gradually add this mixture to the container, stirring slowly and gently.

4. Place container in a protected spot (it must not be moved or touched). Cover with a lid. Cover the container with a large towel or blanket and allow to set at least overnight.

5. To obtain a thick yogurt, place 3–4 layers of paper towels over the top for a few hours to absorb the excess liquid.

6. Store in a refrigerator.

نظر بر روی تو هــر بامداد نوروزی است

شب فراق تو هر شب که هست یلدائی ا

سعدی

Sight of you each morning is a new year
Any night of your departure is the night of yalda.

Sa'di

Winter Festival

شب یلدا

December 21 or 22 is the winter solstice and the longest night of the year. In Iran we call this *Shab-e Yalda*. The ceremony dates back to an Indo-Iranian origin where Light and Good were considered together against Darkness and Evil. This night, the longest in the year, was thought to be extremely unlucky with Evil at the zenith of its powers.

On the *Shab-e Yalda*, fires would be made outside while inside family and friends would gather in a wake around the *corsy*. In the days when fruit and vegetables were available only in season, the host, usually the oldest in the family, would carefully keep grapes, honeydew melons, watermelons and cucumbers. These would then be eaten on this night in a final ceremony of thanks to the fruitful produce of the past year and a prayer for the coming harvest. Pomegranates with *gol-par* (angelica powder) and *Ajeel* are also always a part of this celebration. The family would stay up through the night, the fires burning and the lights lit, helping the sun in its battle against darkness. Keeping each other company, the family would recite poetry, tell jokes and stories, talk and eat, eat and talk until the sun, triumphant, reappeared in the morning.

Note: *Traditionally placed in the family living room, the* corsy *is a low, square table covered with a thick cloth overhanging on all sides. A brazier with hot coals is then placed under the table. In cold winter weather family and friends spend the day and sometimes all night sitting on large cushions (futons) around the* corsy *with their legs underneath the table and the cloth over their laps.*

Ajeel (page 17) is also sometimes called Shab Chareh, which literally means night grazing.

Note: *Shab-e Yalda* literally means birthday night. *Yalda* is the Syriac for birthday. Early Christians took this very ancient Persian celebration to Mithra, God of Light, and made it Christ's birthday. The dates for Christmas have been slightly changed since but many of the concepts remain the same. Cosmically speaking, the winter solstice is also a birthday, the rebirth of the sun. From this day on the northern hemisphere starts to have more and more light and longer and longer days.

'Tis spring, flowers full and happiness in the green-grass vine
All the blossoms are blooming except mine
Loose not heart free spirit on New Year's day
I heard from the lips of a lily today
Do not sing the seven shams this New Year's eve I beg thee
Complaint, curse, corruption, cacophony, clumsiness, chaos
*   and cruelty*
The seven symbols make, of serene greenery, scented hyacinth
*   and sweet apple*
Senged, samanou, salway and song spell.
Send the seven symbols to the table of a lover
Throw the seven shams to the door of an ill wisher.
'Tis New Year's eve, rid the heart of darkness
Eventually this black night will turn to light and brightness
Carry out the New Year tradition and God willing
Bring back the feeling to that of the excellent beginnning.

نوبهاراست و بود پرگل و شاداب چمن   همه گل ها بشگفتند بغیر از گل من

حیف باشد دل آزاده نوروزین   این سن هرورشنیم زربان سوسن

شکوه و شین و شغب شهِّ و شور و شیون   هفت شین را مکن جان من اندر شب عید

سجد و سازو سرود و سَمنو سلوی من   هفت سین پاکن از سبزه و از سنبل و سیب

هفت شین را یکی بفرست دلخواه بِه   هفت سین را بدر خانه بدخواه فکن

Bahar

صبح عیداست بون کن دل این تار   کآخر این شام سیه خانه نما یدروشن

رسم نوروز بجا ی آور و از یزدان خواه   کآورد حالت ما باز به حالی حسن

بهار

The New Year's Celebration

The Iranian New Year (*Norouz*) is always on the first day of spring (March 20 or 21) and corresponds with the rebirth of nature. Although the poet Firdusi tells in the Shahnameh (Book of Kings) of the legendary King Jamshid and the first *Norouz* celebration, many of the rituals go back to at least three thousand years ago.

Norouz ceremonies are symbolic representations of two ancient concepts–End and Rebirth, and Good and Evil. To this day, a few weeks before the new year, Iranians thoroughly clean and decorate their homes. They make new clothes, bake pastries and germinate seeds as a sign of renewal. The ceremonial cloth (*sofreh haft sinn*) is set up in each household. Some people, referred to as *Hadji Firouz*, disguised with makeup and wearing very brightly colored outfits, parade through the streets with tambourines singing and dancing to spread good cheer and the news of the coming new year.

On the eve of the last Wednesday of the year (*Shab-e Chahar Shanbeh Soury,*

Note: Halloween is a celtic variation of "Shab-e Chahar Shanbeh Soury," an ancient Persian fire festival for the hallow.

literally the eve of Red Wednesday), bonfires are lit in public places and people leap over the flames, shouting "*Sorkhie to az man o zardie man az to!*" (literally, "Give me your beautiful red color and take back my sickly pallor!"). In this way with the help of fire and light, symbols of good, we hope to see through this unlucky night—the End of the year.

Traditionally it was believed that the living were visited by the spirits of their ancestors on the last days of the year. Many people, especially children, wrap themselves in shrouds (symbolically enacting the visits of the ancestral spirits). They run through the streets, banging on pots and pans with spoons, beating in the last unlucky Wednesday of the year, while knocking on doors asking for treats. In order to make a wish come true, it is customary to prepare and distribute on this night *Ash-e Reshteh-e Nazri* (Noodle Soup, page 34) and a special Ajeel (called *Ajeel-e Moshgel Goshah*, literally unraveller of difficulties) made by mixing the hearts of seven dried fruits and nuts—pistachio, walnut, hazelnut, pumpkin seed, peach, raisin and fig.

A special cover is spread in every household and on it are placed seven symbols beginning with the letter "S:" *sabzeh* (sprouts), *samanou* (a dish made of wheat germ or lentils), *sib* (apples), *sonbol* (hyacinth), *senjed* (fruit of the jujube), *seer* (garlic), and *somagh* (sumac). These represent the seven good angels, heralds of life and rebirth, health, happiness, prosperity, joy and beauty. Seven has been a sacred number since ancient times in Persia.

Also placed on the table are a copy of the Koran, a volume of the poems of Hafez, some coins, a bitter orange floating in a bowl of water, a bowl of painted eggs, a bowl of milk, goldfish in a bowl of water, a flask of rosewater, an incense burner and seven branches from gnarled trees (olive and pomegranate). Two candelabra holding the same number of candles as there are children in the family are placed on either side of a mirror.

The *sofreh-e haft sinn* is left untouched and the lights are left burning on the last night of the year so that the spirits of the ancestors who visit on this night see the respect offered to them and the prosperity and happiness of their offspring. In return, it is then believed, they will give their blessings for the coming year.

In the past on *Norouz* itself, people would rise very early and make their way to sources of water for purifying rites. Today we simply take a bath and put on new clothes.

Family and friends sit around the *sofreh*, awaiting the transition to the new year (*Tahvil*). Traditional songs are sung and the poems of Hafez and verses from the Koran are recited. After the stroke of the equinox, the oldest person present begins the well-wishing by standing up, giving everyone a sweet pastry, some gold or silver coins and lots of hugs. Calm, happiness, sweetness and perfumed odors are very important on this day of rebirth, as the mood on this day is said to continue through the year. An old saying goes, Good thought, Good word, Good deed–to the year end happy indeed.

Note: The seven s's were originally haft sini (*literally seven dishes); this later became seven sweet things (*haft shin *for* Shirini) *but now most people, except in the very traditional villages, just know it as "haft Sinn." Sprouts and* samanou *represent rebirth – apples and the fruit of the jujube love, beauty and birth. Hyacinths and rosewater are placed for their sweet odors, while wild rue (*espand) *is burned to drive away evil spirits. Fish is the symbol of the astral year end, Pisces. Garlic and sumac represent health – eggs, birth – coins, prosperity and wealth. Orange in a bowl of water is the world floating in space-time, and the gnarled branches our life's passage through it. Candles represent light and all that is good.*

On the thirteenth day of *Norouz*, called *Sizdeh-Bedar*, whole families leave their homes carrying trays of sprouted seeds and form a procession to go to picnic in a cool, grassy place. Far from home, they throw the sprouts into the water completing the process of the end of one year and the rebirth of another. There is much singing and dancing and eating and drinking on this joyful day which marks the end of the *Norouz* celebrations.

Note: One legendary beginning of our calendar is recounted in the Shahnameh by the poet Firdusi. King Jamshid was a wise and capable leader. He made weapons and conquered evil, clothed his people and created a government. He subordinated the *divs* (demons) and used them to build cities. He discovered precious metals and stones and finally built ships and sailed the seas.

When Jamshid had done all this, he decided that he was master of all. Only the heavens remained for him. He ordered a throne to be made of jewels *(Takht-e Jamshid)*. Jamshid sat on his throne and ordered the *divs* to lift him up to the sky. Everyone gathered round and marveled at his blessings and power. They showered him with jewels and called that day *Norouz* (the new day). It was the first day of the year and of spring. On that day the body took respite from work and the heart from hatred. The nobles ordered a celebration with wine and singing.

For three hundred years the people knew nothing of death, hardship or sadness and the *divs* were chained up as slaves. Eventually Jamshid's power corrupted him. Filled with pride he said, "All this have I created. You owe everything to me. I am the Creator." And so he fell from the grace of God and disorder reigned again in the land.

جهان انجمن شد بر تخت او   فروماند از فره ایزد بخت او

به جمشید بر گوهر افشاندند   بر آن روز را روز نو خواندند

شاهنامه فردوسی

New Year's Dinner

Chameh Aid-e Norouz

Fish and noodles are usually served on New Year's. It is believed they bring good luck in the year that lies ahead. The traditional menu usually includes:

Noodle Soup/*Ash-e Reshteh*
Rice with Fresh Herbs and Fish/*Sabzi Polo Ba Mahi*
Herb Kookoo/*Kookoo-ye Sabzi*
Rice with Noodles/*Reshteh Polo*

New Year's Ceremony Setting
Sofreh-e Haft Sinn
page 214

Peasant Wedding Ceremony Setting
Sofreh-e-Aghde
page 217

تا کی غم آن خورم که دارم یا نه
وین عمر بخوبی گذرانم یا نه

پر کن قدح باده که معلومم نیست
کین دم که فرو برم بر آرم یا نه

خیام

Have I enough? Am I secure or not?
Will blessings and my joys endure or not?
Ah, fill my cup with wine–who knows, the breath
Inhaled, I may exhale for sure or not?

Omar Khayyam

Wedding Ceremony

Dressed in white with gold embroidery, the bride sits in front of a mirror framed in silver, gold or crystal and lit by two candelabra, one on either side. According to tradition, the mirror and candlesticks should be gifts from the groom, symbolizing purity and love. When he enters the room where the ceremony will be held, the first thing he sees is the face of his wife-to-be, reflected in the mirror by candlelight.

The *sofreh-e-aghde* (the wedding cloth), a fine hand-sewn *termeh* glittering with gold and silver threads, is spread out before the mirror. Food and objects traditionally associated with marriage are arranged on the *sofreh*. These are:

— an assortment of sweets and pastries prepared in the bride's home but paid for by the bridegroom. Among them are *noghle* (sugar-coated almonds), *nabat* (sugar crystals), *baklava*, *toote* (dried mulberries), *nan-e berenji* (rice cookies), *nan-e nokhodchi* (chick-pea cookies), *nan-e badami* (almond cookies), *goush-e fil* (elephant ears) and *sohan assali* (honey almonds);

— a platter of bread, feta cheese and fresh herbs, which the guests share immediately after the ceremony to bring the new couple happiness and prosperity;

—a basket of raw eggs, symbolizing fertility; a basket of almonds and walnuts in the shell; a bowl of honey (to make the future sweet); two large solid cones of sugar (to be used in the wedding ceremony); fresh flowers in abundance (expressing the hope that beauty will adorn the couple's life together); an open flask of rosewater to perfume the air; a needle and seven strands of different colored threads (to sew up the mother-in-law's mouth if need be); and an open Koran or other holy books.

As the ceremony begins, friends or relatives of the bride hold a square of white silk or cotton over her head, while others rub the cones of sugar together, raining sweet joy and happiness down upon her.

A holy man chosen by the couple recites the traditional prayers. He then asks the bride, "Young and noble woman, do you realize you are marrying an honorable man for this *mahr*?"*

But those in attendance pretend the bride is absent, saying such things as, "She is not here. She went out to gather rosebuds."

The holy man repeats the question three times and the bride finally answers yes. He then declares the couple man and wife. The groom kisses the bride on the forehead, then they each place a *noghle* (sugar coated almond) in the other's mouth. Friends and relatives shower them with more *noghles* and gold or silver coins before offering them their wedding gifts.

The wedding is a splendid affair, held in the home of the groom. A lavish meal is offered, sometimes with a whole roast lamb as the centerpiece. *Shirine polo*, or sugared rice, is always served, along with many other dishes: pastries, sweets, *ajeel* (a mixture of dried fruit and nuts), fresh fruit, hot and cold drinks and, finally, an elaborate wedding cake. The celebration, with so much feasting, singing and dancing, is a day for all to remember.

After the guests have gone home, it is customary to give the remaining pastries to those who were unable to come and to those who helped make the day a success.

*The mahr *is a sum of money, an object of value or a piece of property that the groom agrees to give the bride. It is her financial security in case of marital discord. The bride brings her dowry, or* jahaz, *to her new home. The details of the* mahr *and* jahaz *are spelled out in the* ghabaleh *or marriage contract.*

HOT AND COLD DRINKS

باسا قی آن می که حال آورد   کرامت فـــز ايد كمال آورد

به من ده كه بس بیدل افتاده‌ام   وز این هر دو بحاصل افتاده‌ام

باسا قی آن می كز او جام جم   زند لاف بینائی اندر عدم

به من ده كه گردم به تأیید جام   چو جم اگه از سرّ عالم تمام

Saghi! Come, that wine that rapture bringeth,
Give me. For I, much heart-bereft, have fallen;
Saghi come. That wine, wherefrom the cup of Jamshid,
Boasteth of seeing into non-existence.

Give me, so that by the aid of the cup,
I may be like Jamshid,
Ever acquainted with the world's mystery.

Hafiz – Saghi Nameh

Cold Drinks

One day, as King Jamshid sat under his tent watching his archers practice, a large bird appeared in the sky. It seemed to be struggling to stay aloft. Jamshid saw that a snake was wrapped around the bird's neck, threatening it with its fearsome fangs.

For Jamshid this was a hateful sight. He could not stand by and allow the bird, a symbol of good, to be devoured by a snake, the foulest symbol of evil.

Without hesitation, the king ordered his best archer to kill the snake without harming the bird. A few moments later, the serpent fell to the ground, an arrow through its head.

The great bird soared toward the sun in homage to the triumph of good over evil, then swooped down to alight next to Jamshid. It opened its beak and dropped a few bright green seeds at the king's feet. Jamshid had never seen seeds like these. He looked up to question the bird but it had already flown away.

When the king returned to his palace, he summoned his best gardeners and consulted the wisest men in his kingdom, but not one was able to identify the strange seeds. Finally, he ordered them planted in the most fertile part of the royal gardens.

Some time later, a strange plant rose from the ground. During the warm season it proliferated, sending out long branches covered with many large leaves. But once winter arrived, it seemed to dry up and shrivel to the ground, as if to protect itself from the cold.

Finally, the first of its fruit ripened. A gardener brought them to Jamshid, who examined them in wonder. They were as strange as the plant that bore them. On each stem there grew not one but twenty to forty dark blue, round berries. Their juice began to burst through their delicate skin. So that not a drop would be lost, the king ordered his servants to place the fruit in large receptacles.

One evening the king returned to the palace very thirsty after a long day's hunt in the hot sun. He decided to try a glass of the mysterious juice, believing it would be a refreshing fermented drink. No sooner had he taken the first bitter sip than he spit it out.

"This must be a dreadful poison," he said. "I must make certain it does not fall into the hands of the wrong people."

He turned his attention to more pressing royal concerns and thought no more about the matter. Months passed.

Now as it happened, Jamshid had a beautiful slave girl who had become his favorite. One day while he was away, she fell violently ill, suffering from terrible headaches that none of the palace doctors could cure. The pain was so intense she decided to kill herself. Remembering the strange juice and the king's remark that it was poison, she begged a eunuch to bring a jar of it in secret to her chambers.

She drank one glass and was quite surprised to find that it did not have the bitter taste the king had complained of. To ensure that she would die, she drank a second, then a third glass, and finally fell into a deep sleep.

When she awoke, her terrible headache was gone. Although her mouth felt dry, she believed that she was healed.

When the king returned to the palace, she confessed what she had done and described the miraculous cure the drink had brought about. Because Jamshid loved the beautiful slave girl, he did not punish her. Instead, he asked to try the juice. He tasted it, cautiously at first, then with more and more pleasure. Unable to disguise his delight, he decreed the drink would be used as a remedy for all the people. It was so successful, especially among the elderly, that it came to be called *daroo shah*–the king's medicine.

That, according to legend, is the origin of the grape vine and the discovery of wine.

Cynics will probably question the truth of this tale. It is certain, however, that the grape vine originated in the Middle East and it was there that, one long-forgotten day, the juice of the grapes turned into wine.

The Moslem religion forbids believers to seek paradise on Earth through artificial intoxication. The Koran promises its followers a far more precious nectar—but in the other world.

Over the years, Persians have learned how to concoct a variety of non-alcoholic drinks. These fall into two categories: *afshoreh* and *sharbat*. *Afshoreh* are beverages made from the juice of fresh fruits such as watermelon, pomegranate and orange, squeezed or processed in a blender and served over ice. *Sharbat* are syrups made of fruit juice cooked with sugar and stored in bottles. A little bit of syrup is mixed with water and poured over ice.

زیباترین اشیا ، فکـْزترین اعیان   ازهرچه هست پیدا وزهرچه هست پنهان

ازمرغها هزاراست ، ازوقتها سحرگه   ازفصلها بهاراست ، ازنوعها ست انسان

ازعهد شباب است ، ازآبها شراب است   ازنجم آفتاب است ، ازماهها ست نیسان

ازسنگها دل دوست ، ازعیش ها غم اوست   ازتیغ ها ست ابرو ، ازدشنه ها ست مژگان

اززیب ها ست افسر ، ازطیب ها ست عنبر   ازعضوها ست دیده ، ازخلقها ست احسان

Of things most beautiful of hours most wonderful
Of all that is visible of all that is hidden

Of birds—the nightingale, of time—the dawn
Of seasons—the spring, of species—the human

Of Age it is youth, of liquids it is wine
Of planets our sun, of months the April rain

Of stones—a friend's heart, of pleasures—the pain
Of swords—the eyebrow, of daggers—the eyelash

Of jewels it is the Tiara, of wood it is amber
Of the senses it is sight, of qualities it is virtue

Neshat

Lemon Syrup

Makes 2 pints
Preparation time: 5 min.
Cooking time: 25 min.

1 cup lemon juice
2 cups sugar
3 cups water

GARNISH
   Sprigs of fresh mint
   Lemon or lime slices

Sharbat-e Ablimou

1. Place lemon juice, sugar and water in a saucepan. Bring to a boil and simmer over medium heat about 25 minutes. Cool and pour into a clean bottle.

2. In a pitcher, mix ¼ syrup, ¾ water and 2 ice cubes per person. Stir with a spoon. Serve well chilled.

Variation: In a glass, dissolve 1 tablespoon sugar in a little tap water. Add fresh lemon or lime juice and ice cubes and fill ⅔ way with cold water. Garnish with sprigs of fresh mint and slices of lemon or lime.

Sour-Cherry Syrup

Makes 1 pint
Preparation time: 20 min.
Cooking time: 35 min.

3 cups fresh or frozen pitted sour cherries or canned ones with their juice
2 cups sugar
½ cup water
¼ teaspoon vanilla extract

Sharbat-e Albalou

1. Squeeze or process the cherries in a juicer.

2. Bring the cherry juice, sugar and water to a boil in a saucepan. Simmer for 25 minutes over low heat until the syrup thickens.

3. Remove pan from heat. Add vanilla and allow to cool.

4. Pour syrup into a clean, dry bottle. Cork tightly.

5. In a pitcher, mix ¼ syrup, ¾ water and 2 ice cubes per person. Stir with a spoon. Serve well chilled.

Variation: Another way to make this syrup is to bring the sugar and water to a boil, add the sour cherries and boil for 25 minutes. Remove cherries with a skimmer and add ¼ teaspoon vanilla extract to the syrup. Let cool, pour syrup into a clean, dry bottle and cork tightly.

Quince Syrup

2 large quinces, about 2 pounds
2 pounds sugar
2 cups water
½ cup lime juice

Makes 1 pint
Preparation time: 10 min.
Cooking time: 25 min.

شربت به لیمو

Sharbat-e Beh Limou

1. Quarter the quinces and remove cores with a knife. Wash and pat dry. Process in juicer.

2. Bring sugar and water to a boil in a saucepan. Add quince juice and lime juice and boil for 30 minutes over medium heat until syrup thickens.

3. Remove saucepan from heat. Allow to cool. Pour syrup into a clean, dry bottle and cork tightly.

4. In a pitcher, mix ¼ syrup, ¾ water and 2 ice cubes per person. Stir with a spoon. Serve well chilled.

5. Serve chilled in a glass, with a teaspoon.

Variation: Another way to make this syrup is to bring the sugar and water to a boil and add cored and chopped quince with the lime juice. Simmer for 20 minutes over medium heat, then strain the syrup.

Rhubarb Syrup

1 **pound rhubarb**
1 **cup water**
3 **cups sugar**

Makes 1 pint
Preparation time: 35 min.
Cooking time: 30 min.

Sharbat-e Rivasse

1. Remove strings from rhubarb, wash and cut into 1½-inch pieces. Process in a juicer.

2. Bring the juice, water and sugar to a boil in a saucepan. Boil for 20 minutes over high heat, stirring constantly.

3. Allow to cool. Pour syrup into a clean, dry bottle. Cork tightly.

4. In a pitcher, mix ¼ syrup, ¾ water and 2 ice cubes per person. Stir with a spoon. Serve well chilled.

Variation: To make this syrup without a juicer, bring 1 pound rhubarb, cleaned and cut in chunks, 4 cups of sugar and 2 cups water to a boil in a saucepan. Simmer over medium heat for 30 minutes. Place a strainer over a bowl and pour in the puree. Extract all the syrup by pressing with a wooden spoon. Pour into a clean, dry bottle and cork it. Serve as above.

Rosewater Syrup

Makes 1 pint
Preparation time: 5 min.
Cooking time: 20 min.

1 cup water
2½ cups sugar
¼ cup lemon juice
½ cup rosewater

Sharbat-e Gol-e Sorkh

1. Bring water and sugar to a boil in a saucepan. Simmer 10 minutes. Add lemon juice and rosewater and cook 10 minutes longer.

2. Remove pan from heat and allow to cool. Pour syrup into a clean, dry bottle. Cork tightly.

3. In a pitcher, mix ¼ syrup, ¾ water and 2 ice cubes per person. Stir with a spoon. Serve well chilled.

Note: Rosewater may be purchased in food specialty stores (page 240).

Vinegar Syrup

Makes 1 pint
Preparation time: 5 min.
Cooking time: 35 min.

6 **cups sugar**
2 **cups water**
1½ **cups wine vinegar**
4 **sprigs fresh mint**
1 **cucumber, peeled and grated**

GARNISH
   Lime slices
   Sprigs of mint

Sharbat-e
Sekanjebine

1. Bring sugar and water to a boil in a saucepan. Simmer for 10 minutes over medium heat, until sugar has dissolved.

2. Add vinegar and boil 25 minutes longer over medium heat until a thick syrup forms. Remove saucepan from heat.

3. Wash mint and pat dry. Add it to the syrup. Allow to cool. Remove mint and pour syrup into a clean, dry bottle. Cork tightly.

4. In a pitcher, mix ¼ syrup, ¾ water and 2 ice cubes per person. Add the cucumber and stir well. Pour into individual glasses and decorate each with a slice of lime and a sprig of fresh mint. Serve well chilled.

Yogurt Drink

Makes 2 servings
Preparation time: 10 min.

1 cup thick whole-milk yogurt
   (recipe, page 212)
1 teaspoon chopped fresh mint
   or a dash of dried mint flakes,
   crushed
½ teaspoon salt
¼ teaspoon ground pepper
1½ cups club soda or springwater

Doogh

1. Pour yogurt, mint, salt and pepper into a pitcher. Stir well.

2. Add club soda or springwater gradually, stirring constantly. Add 3 or 4 ice cubes and mix again.

3. Serve chilled.

Tea and Samovar

Chai-o Samovar

In every Iranian household, a *samovar* sits on a large tray with a bowl called the *jaam* under the spout to catch the drips. The teapot, a jar of tea and a covered bowl of sugar are set out beside the *samovar*, which is kept steaming all day long. As soon as a visitor steps over the threshold of a home or office, a small glass of tea with three lumps of sugar and a teaspoon is offered to him. We serve tea in a glass in order to be able to appreciate its color. The color and the fragrance of tea are very important to us, for we believe the pleasures of sight and smell come before that of taste.

Tea is Iran's national drink — and excellent quality tea is grown there. We never drink it with milk. Instead, we take it with sugar or with half a lime, honey, dates, raisins, dried sweet mulberries or even jam instead of sugar. Tea is always served very hot.

Here is how to make a good cup of tea:

1. Boil water in the *samovar*.

2. Warm the teapot with a little boiling water which you throw away into the *jaam*. Add 2 teaspoons of tea leaves to the pot. A 50-50 blend of Earl Grey and Darjeeling teas closely resembles Persian tea.

3. Fill the teapot half-full with boiling water and steep tea for 5 to 10 minutes on top of the *samovar*. Do not let the tea steep for more than 10 minutes; the quality of it will change and you will have to start all over. (To make good tea without a *samovar*, place the filled pot over gentle heat for 5 minutes, then use a tea cozy to keep it warm.)

4. Before serving, pour out a glassful of tea and return it to the pot to make sure the tea is evenly mixed.

5. Fill each glass half way with tea, then add boiling water from the *samovar*. This way the tea can be diluted to a fine color and to taste: some people prefer their tea strong, others weak. Put the teapot back on top of the *samovar* to keep it hot.

قهوه

Coffee

Ghahveh

Iranian coffee is like Turkish coffee, thick and very strong. In fact, in Iran it is called Turkish coffee. It is made from coffee beans ground to a very fine powder and then simmered with sugar. It is usually made in a long handled copper pot shaped like a beaker and then poured into very small cups. It is easy to make:

1. For each small cup, put 1 teaspoon coffee, 1 teaspoon sugar and 1 turkish cup (small cup) water in a Turkish coffeepot. Stir with a spoon.

2. Simmer over low heat until foam rises to the surface. Remove immediately from heat and serve.

Pastries or fruit are always served with this coffee. You have to sip the coffee carefully so as not to swallow any grounds.

After drinking the coffee, remove the saucer and place it on top of the cup. Invert the cup and saucer away from yourself with the left hand (the hand of the heart) and let stand for 10 minutes without disturbing it. Then turn the cup over. A fortune-teller—or just a clever friend—can read your fate in the patterns of the grounds left behind in the cup.

MY MOTHER'S CLASSIFICATION ON "HOT" AND "COLD" FOODS

Recipes in this book present a balanced dish by combining the opposing elements of *"hot"* and *"cold."* It should be noted that spices also play an important roll in their pharmacological qualities rather than their culinary ones.

Meat

Beef, veal	cold
Duck	hot
Hen	hot
Lamb	hot
Red Snapper	hot
All other fish	cold
Rooster	cold
Turkey	cold

Vegetables

Beets	cold
Cabbage	cold
Cardoons	cold
Carrots	hot
Cauliflower	cold
Celery	cold
Corn	hot
Cucumbers	cold
Eggplants	cold
Garlic	hot
Grape leaves	cold
Green beans	cold
Green peas	cold
Green peppers	hot
Lettuce	cold
Mushrooms	hot
Okra	hot
Onions	hot
Potatoes	cold
Pumpkins	cold
Rhubarb	cold
Shallots	hot
Spinach	cold
Tomatoes	cold
Turnips	cold

Cereals and Beans

Barley	cold
Barley flour	cold
Chick-peas	hot
Cornstarch	hot
Kidney beans	cold
Lentils	cold
Mung beans	hot
Pinto beans	cold
Rice	cold
Wheat flour	hot
Yellow fava beans	cold
Yellow split peas	hot

Fruits

Almonds	hot
Apples	hot
Apricots	cold
Barberries	cold
Dates	hot
Figs	hot
Grapefruit	cold
Mangoes	hot
Nectarines	cold
Oranges	cold
Peaches	cold
Pears	neutral
Pistachios	hot
Prunes	cold
Quinces	hot
Raisins and grapes	hot
Sour cherries	cold
Sweet melon	hot
Walnuts	hot
Watermelon	cold

Herbs

Bay leaf	hot
Chives	hot
Coffee	cold
Coriander leaves	cold
Dill weed	hot
Fenugreek	hot
Garden angelica	hot
Marjoram	hot
Mint	hot
Parsley	hot
Tarragon	hot
Tea	neutral
Whole Persian limes	cold

Spices

Cardamom	hot
Cinnamon	hot
Cloves	hot
Cumin	hot
Curry powder	hot
Ginger	hot
Nigella seed	hot
Nutmeg	hot
Pepper	hot
Saffron	hot
Salt	hot
Sumac	cold
Turmeric	hot
Vanilla	hot

Other

Eggs	hot
Feta cheese	neutral
Honey	hot
Lemon juice	cold
Milk	cold
Persian pickles	hot
Pomegranate paste	cold
Rosewater	hot
Sugar	cold
Tamarind	cold
Tomato paste	cold
Unripe grape juice	cold
Vinegar	hot
Whey	hot
Yogurt	cold

K I T C H E N   E Q U I P M E N T

Persian cooking does not require any special kitchen tools or equipment, although a heavy stew pot is essential and an electric rice cooker is helpful. An electric juice-extractor is also helpful for preparing fruit syrups. The well-equipped kitchen should have the following:

Cutting boards for vegetables, meat and fish
Knives for cutting, slicing, filleting, boning and chopping
Fish scaler
Kitchen pin
Saucepans and frying or sauteing pans
Cast-iron pot with a cover
Teflon-lined pot with lid
Terrines
Oven-proof casseroles
Cookie sheets
Wax paper
Ladles
Skimmers/spatulas
Kitchen tongs
Wooden spatula/spoon
Food mill
Spice mill
Coffee mill
Large stainless steel bowl for washing vegetables
Garlic crusher
Salad basket or spinner
Electric rice cooker
Food processor
Blender
Juicer
Electric juice extractor
Cookie cutters
Rosette iron

E Q U I V A L E N T   M E A S U R E M E N T S

U.S.	Equivalents	Metric
1 teaspoon	60 drops	5 ml.
1 tablespoon	3 teaspoons	15 ml.
2 tablespoons	1 fluid ounce	30 ml.
4 tablespoons	¼ cup	60 ml.
5⅓ tablespoons	⅓ cup	80 ml.
8 tablespoons	½ cup	120 ml.
10⅔ tablespoons	⅔ cup	160 ml.
12 tablespoons	¾ cup	180 ml.
16 tablespoons	1 cup or 8 ounces	240 ml.
1 cup	½ pint or 8 fluid ounces	240 ml.
2 cups	1 pint	480 ml.
1 pint	16 ounces	480 ml.
2 pints	1 quart	960 ml. (approx. 1 ltr.)
2 quarts	½ gallon	
4 quarts	1 gallon	3.8 liters

Weight—grams

1 ounce	16 drams	28 grams
1 pound	16 ounces	454 grams
1 pound	2 cups liquid	454 grams
1 kilo	2.20 pounds	1000 grams

Temperature Equivalents: Fahrenheit—Centigrade

Fahrenheit	200°	225°	250°	275°	300°	325°	350°	375°	400°	425°	450°	475°
Centigrade	93°	110°	130°	140°	150°	170°	180°	190°	200°	220°	230°	240°

ESSENTIAL INGREDIENTS FOR A PERSIAN PANTRY

Whenever possible, use fresh herbs, beans, fruits and nuts, which are more and more commonly available in most supermarkets. However, below is a list of some essential ingredients which should be kept in your pantry in the dried form. Make the syrups, jams and pickles from time to time, store in jars and use as needed.

DRIED HERBS

Barg-e boo—bay leaf
Gard-e-limou-omani—dried Persian lime powder
Geshniz—coriander leaves; also called cilantro or chinese parsley
Gol-par—garden angelica
Limou-omani—whole Persian limes
Marzeh—marjoram
Nana—mint
Shambalileh—fenugreek
Shevid—dill weed
Tareh—chives
Tarkhoon—tarragon

DRIED BEANS

Adass—lentils
Baghali—yellow fava beans
Jow—barley
Lapeh—yellow split peas
Loubia chiti—pinto beans
Loubia ghermez—kidney beans
Nokhod—chick-peas

SPICES

Advieh—a mixture of seasonings (see page 160); allspice may be substituted for it.
Darchin—cinnamon
Hel—cardamom
Jowz-e-hendi—nutmeg
Kari—curry powder
Mikhak—cloves
Siah Daneh—nigella seed
Somagh—sumac
Vanille—vanilla
Zaffaran—saffron

Zanjebil—ginger
Zard-chubeh—turmeric
Zeereh—cumin

OTHER

Ab goureh—unripe grape juice
Ablimou—lemon juice
Basmati—long-grain rice
Golab—rosewater
Kashke—whey powder
Piaz—onions
Roghan zeitoun—olive oil
Seer—garlic
Serkeh—vinegar
Torshi—Persian pickles (see page 164)

PASTES

Rob-e gojeh farangi—tomato paste
Rob-e-anar—pomegranate paste

SYRUPS AND JAMS

Khoshab-e poosteh-porteghal—orange-peel syrup (see page 160)
Moraba-ye albalou—sour-cherry jam
Sekanjebine—vinegar syrup

DRIED FRUITS, FLOWERS AND NUTS

Alou—dried prunes
Barg-e gole-e sorkh—rose petals
Gerdou—walnuts
Gheisi—dried apricots
Keshmesh—raisins
Khalal-e-badam—almond slivers
Khalal-e-pesteh—pistachio slivers
Khorma—dates
Zereshke—barberries

PERSIAN – ENGLISH GLOSSARY

A

Ab goureh—unripe grape juice

Ablimou—lime or lemon juice

Advieh—a mixture of seasonings, including rosepetals, cinnamon, cardamom, black pepper, angelica, nutmeg and cumin (see page 160 for ratio blend); allspice may be substituted for it.

Afshoreh—a non-alcoholic beverage made from the juice of fresh fruits such as watermelon, pomegranates or oranges, and squeezed or processed in a blender and served over ice

Ajeel—a mixture of raisins, nuts and seeds

Albalou—sour cherries

Alou zard—greengage plums

Ashe—soup

B

Baghali—lima beans

Balal—charcoal-roasted corn on the cob

Bamieh—okra

Barg-e boo—bay leaf

Beh—quince

C

Chai—tea

Chelo—cooked plain rice

Corsy—traditionally placed in the family living room, the corsy is a low, square table covered with a thick cloth overhanging on all sides. A brazier with hot coals is then placed under the table. In cold winter weather family and friends spend the day and sometimes all night sitting on large cushions (futons) around the corsy with their legs underneath the table and the cloth over their laps; eating, drinking and chatting; reading, reciting poetry and sometimes playing footsie—enjoying the cozy warmth. Today a small electric space heater can be effectively used instead of the brazier and a television often replaces the poetry.

D

Daneh-e Khashkhash—poppy seeds

Dolmeh—cooked vegetables or vine leaves stuffed with any mixture of meat, rice and herbs

Donbalan—Lamb fries

Doogh—a yogurt drink with mint

F

Farvardin—the first month of the Persian year

G

Garmi—hot (nature or metabolism)

Gerdoo—walnuts

Geshniz—coriander; also called cilantro or Chinese parsley

Ghabaleh—marriage contract

Ghahoot—sweetened roasted chick-pea powder

Gheimeh—small cubes of meat sauteed in oil and seasoned

Ghormeh—meat chunks sauteed in oil with seasoning, for keeping available in the refrigerator

Gojeh sabz—unripe plums

Gol-par—garden angelica

Golab—rosewater
Ghoureh—unripe grapes
Gusht-e kubideh—a paste of cooked meat
  and vegetables

H

Hadji firouz—town clowns
Haft sinn—the seven items beginning with
  the letter "s" set out for the New Year's
  Celebration
Halva—saffron cake
Hel—cardamom

J

Jafary—parsley
Jahaz—the bride's dowry
Jo—barley
Jowz-e hendi—nutmeg

K

Kabab—lamb brochettes
Kangar—cardoons
Kashke—whey
Khiar—cucumber
Khoresh—a stew of meat or poultry with
  vegetables and/or fruit and nuts
Kookoo—a vegetable or meat dish with
  beaten eggs oven-baked in a casserole dish

L

Laboo—cooked red beet
Lapeh—yellow split peas
Lavashak—plum paste rolls
Limou-omani—Persian limes
Loubia chiti—pinto beans
Loubia ghermez—kidney beans

M

Mahr—a sum of money, piece of property or
  object of value a groom agrees to give to his
  bride as financial security in case of marital
  discord

Marzeh—marjoram
Mash—mung beans
Mey—wine
Meygou—shrimp
Mikhak—cloves
Miveh—fruit
Mokhalafatte—appetizers and condiments
Moraba—jams or preserves
Mosama—a rich, unctuous stew
Musir—shallots

N

Nabat—sugar crystals
Nan—bread
Nana—mint
Noghle—sugar-coated almonds
Nokhod—chick-peas
Norouz—New Year's Day; the Iranian year
  begins on March 20 or 21, the first day of
  spring

P

Panir—feta cheese
Pesteh—pistachios
Piazcheh—scallion
Polo—cooked rice
Poost-e porteghal—orange peel

R

Rayhan—basil
Reshteh—noodles
Rivasse—rhubarb
Rob-e anar—pomegranate paste

S

Sabzeh—sprouts
Sabzi-khordan—green herbs
Samovar—metal urn with a heating device
  for heating water in order to make tea and
  be able to keep the teapot on top brewing
  throughout the day
Sardi—cold (nature or metabolism)

Sekanjebin—vinegar syrup

Senjed—fruit of the jujube tree

Serkeh—vinegar

Shab-charreh—*ajeel*, a mixture of nuts, dried fruits and seeds, which literally means night grazing

Shab-e Yalda—the longest night of the year; the winter solstice

Shahnameh—The Book of Kings, by the poet Firdusi

Shambalileh—fenugreek

Sharbat—syrups made of fruit juice cooled with sugar and stored in bottles

Shewid—dill

Siah-daneh—nigella seeds or black caraway

Sirab shirdoun—tripe

Sobhaneh—breakfast

Sofreh—a cotton cloth embroidered with prayers and poems that serves as a tablecloth on a table or Persian carpet

Sofreh-e haft sinn—the necessary elements laid out on a tablecloth for the New Year's celebration

Sofreh-e-aghde—cloth used in wedding ceremony

Somagh—sumac

T

Tah chin—lamb or chicken slices arranged on the bottom of a pan with rice

Tah digue—a layer of golden rice that sticks to the bottom of the saucepan when rice is cooked

Tanour—bread oven

Tareh—chives

Tarkhoon—tarragon

Toote—mulberries

Torshi—Persian pickles

V

Vanille—vanilla

Z

Zaban—tongue

Zafaran—saffron

Zanjebil—ginger

Zard-chubeh—turmeric

Zeereh—cumin

Zereshke—barberries

SPECIALTY STORES

United States

East

Asia Center
303 West Broad Street
Route 7
Falls Church, VA 22046
(703) 533-2112

Cardullo's Gourmet Shop
6 Brattle Street
Cambridge, MA 02138
(617) 491-8888

Dokan-Deli
7921 Old Georgetown Road
Bethesda, MD 20814
(301) 657-2361

International House
765-H Rockville Pike
Rockville, MD
(301) 279-2121

International Market & Deli
2010 P Street, NW
Washington, DC 20007
(202) 293-0499

Karnig Tashjian Corporation
380 Third Avenue
New York, NY 10016
(212) 683-8458

Mediterranean Deli
81 North Glebe Road
Arlington, VA 22203
(703) 527-0423

Model Food Importers and Distributors
113-115 Middle Street
Portland, ME 04111
(207) 774-3671

Near East Market
602 Reservoir Avenue
Cranston, RI 02910
(401) 941-9763

Sahadi Importing Company
187-189 Atlantic Avenue
Brooklyn, NY 11201
(718) 624-4550

South

Angel's Market
455 Athens Street
Tarpon Spring, FL 33589
(813) 937-6751

West

Ahvaz International Groceries
2133 West Lincoln Avenue
Anaheim, CA 92801
(714) 772-4492

Akoubian's Deli-Grocery
16535 Brookhurst Street
Westminster, CA 92683
(714) 775-7977

Ara Deli
1021 East Broadway
Glendale, CA 91205
(818) 241-2390

Attari
1398 Westwood Boulevard
West Los Angeles, CA
(213) 474-6023

Beverly Square Market
9238 West Pico Boulevard
Los Angeles, CA 90035
(213) 278-6329

City Market
4948 El Cajon Boulevard
San Diego, CA 92115
(619) 583-5811

Elat Market
893 West Pico Boulevard
Los Angeles, CA 90035
(213) 273-0862

International Jr. Market
67114 Reseda Boulevard
Reseda, CA 91335
(818) 342-9753

Jojono's
8801 Reseda Boulevard
Reseda, CA 91335
(818) 993-7064

Lida's Food Center
1842 North Tustin Avenue
Orange, CA 92665
(714) 998-7760

Middle East Market
2054 San Pablo
Berkeley, CA 94702
(415) 548-2213

Miller's Market
17261 Vanowen
Van Nuys, CA 91406
(818) 345-9222

Sam's Food Market
4356 Sepulveda Boulevard
Culver City, CA 90230
(213) 390-5705

Star Market
12134 Santa Monica Boulevard
West Los Angeles, CA 90025
(213) 820-6513

Westwood Grocery
2091 Westwood Boulevard
Westwood, CA 90025
(213) 475-9804

Canada

A & A Foods
266 Elgin Street
Ottawa
(613) 737-2144

Ayoub's Fruits & Vegetable Market
322 Somerset East (at Bleckburn)
Ottawa
(613) 233-6417

Domestic Foods
595 Gladstone
Ottawa
(613) 236-6421

Sayfy's Groceteria
265 Rue Jean Talon Est
Montreal
(514) 277-1257

Main Importing Grocery, Inc.
1188 Boulevard Saint Laurent
Montreal
(514) 861-5681

England

Five Continents
67 Westbourne Grove
London W 2
(01) 229-7255

I N D E X